# LETTERS FROM JERUSALEM

## 1947-1948

"A magnificent book. . .exciting, inspiring, filled with idealism and humor."

"A brilliant insight of life in Israel during the transitional period of the country's War of Independence. A must for all students of Israeli society, past and present."

"A riveting account. . .in a way more meaningful and understandable than a historical, political or military record."

"The true test of the book's quality is its relevance today."

"Chunks of genuine history, dipped into the deep freezer 40 years ago and now defrosted for the reader of today, in all their original freshness."

"A fascinating book. . ."

"What makes this slim volume so memorable is its evocation of the fervor of the State's early days. . . .An experience not to be missed."

"A marvelous way for teenagers to intimately experience this pivotal period of Jewish history."

"The bare facts of history are fleshed out with warmth and color in these letters home."

"Compulsory reading because of both its historic and human content."

"These letters remain as moving and vivid as if written last week."

"This blow by blow account. . .offers all those who missed it a chance to be in Jerusalem of 1947-48."

# Letters from
# Jerusalem

## 1947 - 1948

by Zipporah Porath

Temple Israel
Scranton, Pennsylvania USA
5758/1998

# Temple Israel
## 918 East Gibson Street
## Scranton, Pennsylvania 18510
## USA

Rabbi David Geffen, Ph.D.
Marshall Wolkenstein, Cantor
Joseph Hollander, President

Phone: (717) 342-0350
Fax: (717) 342-7250
Website: www.ncx.com/wwi/tis
e-mail: tiscran@epix.net

First published in Israel.
Second edition. Published by Temple Israel, Scranton, Pennsylvania USA in 1998.

ISBN: 965-222-110-4
Printed in the United States of America

*For Gideon, Tami, Maya and Daria*
*Jonathan and Basmat*

---

*This book would not have come into being*
*without the unfailing encouragement and*
*devotion of my late husband, Joseph.*

# Table of Contents

As we approach the 50th anniversary of the establishment of the State of Israel, there is good cause to look at the events which took place between 1947 and 1948 as a miracle of the modern age. These events continue to fascinate and inspire Jews throughout the world. In a real sense it is a modern-day equivalent to the exodus from Egypt. The great majority of Jews alive today did not have the opportunity to participate actively in the founding of the Jewish State. Thus, we pay great respect to these accomplishments, the fruits of which continue to be enjoyed by all Jewish people.

While historians can write about events that took place 50 years ago, the letters which Zipporah Borowsky Porath wrote to her parents and sister during that memorable year, give us a first-hand account from an American who actually experienced history in the making. Her letters tell the story as an eyewitness, and thus present an account that has the freshness of a current news bulletin. It is the next best thing to being there!

Temple Israel of Scranton is very pleased to be publishing these letters which certainly provide new and personal insights to the beginning of Israeli statehood. We feel these "Letters from Jerusalem" will tell the story of Israel's founding to a new generation of Jews much as a Haggadah tells of the exodus from biblical times.

We are most appreciative to Mr. & Mrs. Norman Aerenson, Mr. & Mrs. Myer Alperin, Mrs. Yetta Chaiken, Mr. & Mrs. David Epstein, The Gelb Foundation, Mr. & Mrs. Saul Kaplan and Mr. & Mrs. Bernard Siegel, who made this printing possible.

It is our fervent hope that Zippy Porath's story will instill in Jews of future generations the Zionist commitment of which she is a splendid example.

*Richard S. Bishop*
Chairman, Publication Committee
Past President, Temple Israel of Scranton

I have been in Israel from the moment — and even before — this fragile state gulped its first independent breath and proclaimed to the world that it had come into existence.

When I came, I had no way of knowing that I would arrive in the Holy Land at the right moment in history; that 1947–48 would be a fateful year; that I would be caught up in Israel's War of Independence, join the Haganah, serve as a nurse and live through the siege of Jerusalem. Nor could I have known that the State of Israel would come into being. I had left America for what was supposed to be only a year of study at the Hebrew University. It turned out to be a year that changed my whole life.

The letters I wrote to my family from Jerusalem and other cities were treasured and preserved by my parents. I was to find the frayed packet nearly four decades later, after their deaths, reread what I had written then and realize that these letters vividly recapture — not only for my own children and grandchildren but for others as well — the incredible ecstasy of being part of statehood-in-the-making: the privilege, pride, euphoria, bravery and bloodshed that is now their heritage. I told it as I saw it happen. I was there!

* * *

Before the State of Israel came into being, getting into the Holy Land was even harder than staying there. The British, who ruled the country under a mandate from the League of Nations, rigidly restricted the number of Jews allowed in, although they were solemnly pledged to encourage the establishment in Palestine of a National Home for the Jewish people. If, however, you were a student who had been admitted to a recognized institution of higher learning (there were only two in Palestine at that time) you stood a fair chance of getting an entry permit. That's how I came.

I landed in Haifa even before the following item appeared on October 17, 1947 in the *New Palestine*, a periodical published by the Zionist Organization of America and widely read by American Zionists:

### SCHOLARSHIP WINNERS LEAVE FOR PALESTINE

Among the passengers on the American liner the *Marine Jumper* when it left New York recently enroute to Palestine were Zipporah Borowsky and Carmi Charney, both of whom are going to study at the Hebrew University in Jerusalem for a year under a scholarship granted to them by the Zionist Organization of America.

Actually, I hadn't intended to go at that time. I had a terrific job producing program material for a network of community centers (YMHAs) throughout the United States, was enjoying an active social life and had just been elected president of a prestigious district of the Zionist Organization of America.

So why pack my bags and go off to ports unknown? I suspect it had something to do with my father, who was a renowned Hebraist and Jewish educator and a prominent Zionist leader in America. He applied for this scholarship on my behalf and then prodded me to go for the interview. Nobody was more surprised than I at being selected.

To go or not to go: how could I turn it down? A year's paid tuition at the Hebrew University and a hard-to-get valid entry visa to British Mandatory Palestine offered to me on a silver platter. Here was a chance to stop talking about being a Zionist and get to *Eretz Yisrael* (the Land of Israel) to see for myself what it was all about. I should also mention I had never been abroad. In my circles major traveling was done on buses and subways commuting between Brooklyn, Manhattan and the Bronx.

Amidst a whirlwind departure, filled with frantic last-minute arrangements, shopping and farewell parties, I managed to make it to the pier on time. The family album features a picture of my mother, father and sister Naomi, taken just as I boarded the ship on September 26, 1947, with me wearing a stunning white suit and white wool coat, looking as if I were leaving on a Mediterranean cruise. I never again got to wear any of those clothes.

As I stood at the ship rail watching my family and friends disappear from view, I tried my best to put out of my mind the fearful thoughts that popped into it and the lump of emotion that gripped me. I was leaving home for the first time, headed for a country beset by troubles. I was going to Jerusalem, the cradle of Jewish civilization; and to British Mandatory Palestine where the cradle was being rocked convulsively.

*Zipporah Porath*

## Part One

# First Encounters

*September 28, 1947*

Dearest Mother, Dad and Naomi,

First day at sea and all's well. Leaving your waving handkerchiefs behind, the boat made a mad dash from Pier 84 out into New York Harbor, only to anchor there stockstill till after midnight, literally hitched to the Statue of Liberty. Apparently, something went wrong with the engine or the electricity. There were even rumors that we might have to turn around and head back to starting point, but thanks to the good old U.S. Navy we were fixed up shipshape and set out for rough waters.

Breakfast this morning consisted of watery eggs and, if your boardinghouse reach was long enough, muffins and something black the Brazilians would never have recognized as coffee. The sun is trying very hard to stay out but the odds are against it and it'll probably duck under the next cloud. It is approximately 10:30 in the morning and seventeen more days of this inactivity will surely drive me over the rail.

I don't know what I expected from this old tug, the *Marine Jumper*. It's a reconditioned U.S. Army troopship making its postwar maiden voyage. The passengers are an odd mixture of everything Middle Eastern and down under, including Arabs from Lebanon, Syria and Egypt, Greeks, Turks, Jews, and lots of unidentifiables. There are plenty of babies and toddlers scrambling about. In fact I'm blessed with a five-month old right under my bunk. He was all right last night, or at least I slept through it, but early this morning he started cooing, belching and gurgling. I think he felt abandoned by his mother in the lower berth

3

who had left him in a crib blocking up the aisle. I came in later than I should have and had a heck of a time trying to climb into bed without waking mama or the baby or breaking my neck. Apparently, somebody had taken away the ladder and hidden it.

Just returned after being summoned to receive a parcel. A most lovely basket of flowers, gladiolas, roses, you name it, all draped with ribbons and bows. Somebody was sure glad to see me leave. I distributed as much as I could to the ship's personnel and the rest I expect to smell till they or I expire. Maybe the purser will exchange one for a cabin with only six passengers — if I discuss it with him in person. Am taking the idea under consideration.

*Several days later. . .*

After my experience of the first unrestful night bunked with twenty strange females and a babe in the aisle with not a drop of air to spare, I decided to brave the open spaces and made my way to the sun deck for sleeping quarters. It wasn't half bad; several others had the same idea. Wrapped in blankets, we slept fitfully staring at a sky full of stars and a big beautiful moon. The tossing and rolling of the ship seemed more a lullaby than a punishment and I thanked heaven for my unconventional soul. What would they have said in New England about sleeping in the great outdoors with a pack of strange men? Dawn came up just as the crew arrived to wash the deck.

I think I am beginning to acquire sea legs, whatever they are. I roll at the right moments and toss with the movement of the ship, one sway and we all sway . . .

Was interrupted for a fire drill. Six clangs and a mad rush to your bunk for a life belt, then measured calm while you climb the stairs to the deck and search for the right lifeboat. There was little talk, just the shuffling and

4

scurrying of two thousand feet, everybody hoping that this was just a rehearsal and not the real thing.

Aside from lazing about on the deck, there is little to do. No chairs to be had so between relaxing snoozes we sit propped up back to back or sprawled heads pillowed on stomachs, bodies crisscrossed to form a mass mold of protoplasm — and what we do is a lot of talking. We discuss earth-shaking problems — trying to avoid politics — read poetry and sing. I've learned a saucy song in Arabic and taught my friend Eddie the Arab a popular Hebrew ditty. And that's the routine both day and night. Mealtimes are the interlude between these sessions and they are hurried affairs because the air in the cafeteria is musty and not pleasant.

There are about twenty in our student group, aside from Carmi Charney, the other Zionist Organization scholarship winner traveling with me [who has since done us proud by becoming a prominent Hebrew poet, editor and translator, better known as T. Carmi].* Most are ex-servicemen — a few with wives — approved by the Veterans Administration to study at the Hebrew University in Jerusalem under the GI Bill of Rights. Under the same arrangement, a group of GIs of Lebanese extraction are headed for the American University in Beirut. They are excellent shipmates and I expect they'll come to visit us in Jerusalem during vacation. There is also a small student group going to missionary stations in Beirut and Alexandria, as well as several non-GI students who will also be at the Hebrew University. [My shipmates included Eliezer Whartman, Dave and Chaya Solomon and others.]

---

* Phrases in parentheses are part of the original letters; those in brackets were added during preparation of the manuscript to help the present-day reader. — ED.

This morning we had a cultural interlude. Professor Aryeh Tartakower of the Hebrew University, who is accompanying our group, suggested a *sicha* (discussion) so we went into seclusion for two hours and talked about the Jewish cultural contribution to Palestine during the past ten years. The Beirut University crowd also have occasional lectures.

*More days later. . . you lose track of time*

Gibraltar was a real thrill. We had seen nothing but water, water and more water for days, the endless expanse of an ocean. Then out of the mist — land. Africa on the one side, Europe on the other. We hugged the European side. The two merged in a breathtaking moment and then The Rock came into view, just like Prudential Life Insurance ads. The water was soft as cotton after Gibraltar and the ship glided along effortlessly, bypassing Pantelleria and Crete, and finally arrived in Beirut. We had to remain on the ship overnight in Beirut: there were no shore passes for Jews, who are strictly taboo in Lebanon. From what I saw, the port looked dirty and uninviting but I was told that inland the country is lovely.

Abandoning this for the time being . . . Will have to continue after we land in Haifa.

*Zippy*

---

*Haifa*

*October 13, 1947*

Dear Everybody,

I keep pinching myself just to make sure that I am really here. Am sitting in a modern hotel room and through the window across the street I can see the Technion building and, rising up behind it like a stage backdrop, majestic Mount Carmel. It feels as if picture postcards are parading all around me.

After seventeen days at sea we finally reached Haifa last night but weren't permitted to disembark until 9:00 this morning. Apparently, the ship landed about ten minutes after the Customs House closed, a very frustrating experience to be so near and yet so far. A representative from the Hebrew University was on the pier to give us a royal welcome and steer us through Customs. It seems we'll have to remain in Haifa overnight to clear trunks and large items tomorrow.

After the continuous strain of little sleep, and none at all last night, I am very tired, but that doesn't dull the thrill of being here. It's not just the normal amount of travel excitement at finding yourself in a new place and meeting interesting people. It's an awareness of something much deeper that I sensed the minute I came ashore, watching the stevedores unloading the ship. They formed a human chain and tossed the heavy baggage from hand to hand, all the while calling out to each other in Hebrew. Strong, rowdy, muscle-men, dressed in grubby khaki shorts — a new kind of Jew for me.

Have to stop. Carmi and Al Yanow (the University's representative) are waiting for me to join them for dinner, my first meal in Palestine and my first decent one in two days. I've been too excited to eat. That's it for now.

Love,
*Zippy*

*October 15, 1947*

Dear All,

Taking up where I left off, my first meal in Palestine was at the Haifa *Mitbach Hapoalim* (Workers' "Kitchen"/ Restaurant). I had a little trouble with the menu and have no idea what I ate except that it was filling, fattening and foreign. Afterwards I gave most of it back, probably a reaction to all the excitement of departure and arrival. Instead of joining my shipmates to see the sights, I fell asleep and dreamt about Jewish porters, Jewish waiters and Jewish street beggars all speaking Hebrew. Next day, after another grueling session in Customs, we signed out of the hotel and set out for Jerusalem.

The Jewish cooperative bus company, Egged, is delightfully informal, a pleasant surprise. There were about twenty-five of us going to Jerusalem so Egged provided a "special" at no extra cost to deliver us and our small personal baggage door-to-door; something the 79th Street Crosstown would never have done.

We were stopped twice on the roads by British "Tommies" for examination of passports. I didn't realize we were coming into an armed camp setup and couldn't understand why we were suspect. But I've since discovered that everybody is suspect and searches, curfews and arms requisitions are everyday occurrences in Palestine under British Mandatory rule.

Our Egged driver was a very cheerful fellow who offered a lot of information, even stopping the bus occasionally to point out spots of interest — a hasty glimpse of settlements that until now were only names to me — Binyamina, Hadera, Raanana, Petah Tikvah and Tel

Aviv. I sat directly behind him and heard a lot of interesting mumbling to himself that the others missed. He took so much time for sightseeing that we became alarmed about arriving in Jerusalem in time. The British have imposed a curfew on interurban travel after 6:00 P.M. In the twilight, as we rounded the first of the winding, spiraling hills on the ascent to Jerusalem, I saw a breathtaking, awesome, unforgettable sight: sunset in the Holy Land. I began to feel the reality of being in *Eretz Yisrael.*

Arrangements had been made for us to stay at Pension Pax in the Montefiore District, or Kiryat Moshe as it is called. It's an attractive rooming house rented by the University for students, in this case exclusively American students. As far as I was concerned that meant I wouldn't be hearing much Hebrew. There was no one to protest to, so this morning I scouted around trying to discover where the local students are billeted. Not far away I found a brand new building, modern and clean with large rooms, simply but neatly furnished. In one of the rooms there was a British girl who hadn't yet been assigned a roommate. So, with her permission, I promptly got friends to help move my things and carried out an extremely successful coup d'etat, leaving the formalities for later.

I spent the afternoon unpacking and finding my way about. Also purchased a hot plate to set up minor housekeeping, even though by house rules it is strictly prohibited. This evening finds me comfortably installed in room number 30 in a "pension" which has no address because it isn't on anything resembling a street. It has risen boldly in the middle of nowhere from a pile of earth and rock and dominates the area.

I should explain that a pension is a kind of European-type rooming house. Ours is a three-story building — rather high as houses in Palestine go. Our room is on the top floor where there are only four rooms; the rest of the space is allocated to a huge balcony. This, is in addition to the small one that adjoins each room. None of the houses in Jerusalem have built-in closets so a large portion of a room is filled with a free-standing bulky wardrobe. I'm sure the building will be hell in winter, especially when it rains. It is so isolated and exposed and, of course, there's no central heating.

This evening while my roommate Rae was at a concert, I entertained my movers and invited the next door neighbors in number 29 to join us. They told us they had just returned to their studies after serving for four years in the British Army as Jewish volunteers from Palestine. One is a French-speaking scholar who earns his way teaching Arabic in the secondary school system; his roommate is a blue-blooded third-generation Sabra (native-born Palestinian Jew) majoring in Zoology.

There may be literally oceans between us, but don't waste worry on me. Adjusting to the Levantine life, food, climate, different ways of doing almost everything, and even living in a new language will surely be difficult but, I hope, not devastating. The fact is I'm doing fine. What is hard is to convey to you impressions which I haven't yet assimilated myself.

I can only tell you that in a little less than two days I feel a real sense of belonging here, thanks mainly to my Hebrew, which is good enough so that I can talk with those around me and have immediate rapport. But more important, I feel connected, a link in a long chain of history that has its roots here.

Till further notice, write to me c/o the Hebrew University on Mount Scopus.

Lots of love,
*Zippy*

*October 20, 1947*

Dearest All,

Regards from Henry Wallace [former vice-president of the United States]. I was at the Eden Hotel last night with a reporter for the local English-language paper and some other journalist friends when an impromptu press conference was called because Wallace happened to be staying at the hotel.

He'll never remember what I looked like, but I can tell you he appeared tired and haggard after his trip. Nevertheless, he was very cordial and pleasant to everyone. I was so excited at meeting my first celebrity that I don't recall much of what he said, except the line that will probably make the front page of the *New York Times*: "There is no peace for the world without peace in Palestine." When he heard that the American student group included ex-GIs, he invited us all for breakfast the day after tomorrow.

This morning, I went up to Mount Scopus to see the Hebrew University campus and find out about registration procedures. It is a breathtakingly beautiful place, the highest spot in Jerusalem. On one side, looking past the amphitheater, you can see clear to the Dead Sea; on the other, as if from a low-flying plane, spread out before you is the Old City, the City of King David, looking like a medieval fortress, while outside the ancient walls is the other Jerusalem, the New City, with a golden stone face glistening in the sun.

I found out that I can't hope to complete a master's degree unless I take certain prescribed courses in a major subject that doesn't particularly appeal to me. Rather than do what most Americans do, spend a year studying the language privately, not attending classes, I've decided to take a special course which is being offered in Hebrew — about eighteen hours a week — tailored to the needs of foreign students. It includes several hours a week on Sociology of the Jews, History of the Jews in Modern Times, Geography of Palestine, Literature, Demography, the Development of Jewish Ethics, Talmud, etc. It seems to be a very well-rounded program.

I can't imagine how I will get much studying done in this congenial atmosphere. In the last hour or so, for example, at least ten people have popped in and out of the room to say hello, borrow a book, listen to the radio (most people don't have one), drink tea and try out their English. One guy just felt sick and wanted to be near somebody who looked in better condition. Most of us newcomers succumb, sooner or later, to the misery of *shilshul* (acute diarrhea), which puts you out of commission for anything but running. We are told to beware of water, milk and fruits, but I haven't figured out if that applies to all of them together or each eaten separately in that dangerous order. Somebody should have told us to bring along canned foods. That's the most expensive food item here, and the one least likely to be contaminated.

The other stomach-upsetting matter is the political situation. According to the Mandate, the British are supposed to keep order, but they aren't doing it. There are "incidents" almost every evening but we don't get to find out what happened until the following morning. Most times it's nothing but a siren exercise to keep the tension mounting, and the "all clear" sounds about half an hour later.

Last night, for example, *Etzel* (*Irgun Zevai Leumi*, a militant extremist movement operating independently of the official Jewish organizations) strung up a banner on the corner of Jaffa Road and King George V Street declaring against the partition of Palestine, with explosives attached to both ends so that anyone trying to dismantle it would be blown to smithereens. It took the British police an agonizingly long time to defuse them. For a change, the report about the incident reached us even before the "all clear" was heard.

It's amazing how wide awake people here look at 6:00 A.M. and how many are up and buzzing about at that hour. Makes me feel like I've been missing out on something all my life sleeping until 7:00.

Don't mistake so much letter writing as a sign of homesickness. Not true. Everything is super. Among the American students are several former neighbors from Brooklyn and Manhattan and Zionist youth group friends whose families you know, including Morty Chertoff, Ezra, Skippy, Danny and Alizah Spicehandler, Aryeh Fishman and Sally Horowitz, to mention only a few. Also Rachie Lev, whose brother Aryeh, the Chief Chaplain of the U.S. Army, you probably know. My only complaint is that it is natural for us to switch to English when no one else is around and I feel guilty speaking English in the Holy Land. I guess it will bother me less once school starts.

Love,
*Zippy*


*Jerusalem*

*October 22, 1947*

Dear All,

Am just beginning to get the swing of things here — like learning to order a meal in the local lingo; my biblical

Hebrew is rather quaint and not very functional if you want to eat anything interesting.

What I already really miss are some of the comforts of home, like HOT WATER. Yesterday, I had my first real shower/bath since landing — and that by the sweat of my own brow. You won't believe this, but to warm the water I had to build a wood fire at the bottom of the boiler. It took me half an hour, but was well worth the effort.

Jerusalem is thick with barbed wire and barricades. I registered at the American Consulate and had to go through the business of British-controlled security zone passes and identity inspection. I still haven't gotten used to the idea of being frisked every time I go into a public building, even the Post Office. Seems senseless to me. Anybody who really wanted to blow up the place wouldn't walk through the front door in broad daylight, more likely he'd toss a grenade through the window.

It's just that the British are jittery — and rightly so — because despite their declared mandate to help create a Jewish National Home, they have bowed to Arab pressure and are barring Jewish immigration and denying Jewish national rights. Jews are not permitted to bear arms in their own defense — *on penalty of death* — nor to protect their lives and property against Arab violence. Small wonder that the Jewish community secretly — which is no secret — began to develop its own security setups, first Watchmen, now Home Guard units and Haganah.

The extreme activists, the Irgun (*Etzel*) and the Stern Gang (*Lechi*), are fed up with the policy of passive resistance adopted by the official heads of the *Yishuv* (the Jewish community in Palestine) and are escalating sabotage and retaliation to a high pitch.

To protect themselves, the British have divided the city into security zones — called A, B, and C — and have barricaded themselves behind barbed wire. They venture forth to send trigger-happy Tommies to patrol the streets and armed columns to descend on Jewish settlements in nerve-racking searches for forbidden arms. And, when called upon to protect Jews from an Arab onslaught, stand by vigilantly, enforcing a policy of rigid non-intervention. So who can sleep peacefully at night?

I am hungry for news of the rest of the world. I read the Hebrew press with difficulty and the English news-paper, the *Palestine Post* [now the *Jerusalem Post*], is only four pages in all. Can you imagine trying to squeeze the entire universe, along with events in Palestine, into four measly pages? Any chance of a subscription to the Sunday edition of the *New York Times*?

Love,
*Zippy*

*Jerusalem*

*October 26, 1947*

Dear Mother, Dad and Naomi,

I went to Tel Aviv for the first time the other day — without realizing that I had picked the wrong day. Friday is only half a day in this country. The last bus leaves at 3:30 P.M. so as to arrive back in Jerusalem before the onset of Shabbat, which didn't leave me much time to get acquainted with the first-ever all-Jewish city in modern times. Also, I had a satchel full of parcels foisted on me by friends in the States before I left to deliver to other people's relatives. How could I refuse? Some day I may be on the receiving end.

Tel Aviv is a far cry from provincial Jerusalem, very sophisticated and cosmopolitan with a slight Hebrew accent. The tree-shaded streets are lined with elegant shops and open-air cafes. It has a carnival air about it: big signs, blaring noises, laughing faces, boisterous children and flamboyant colors. Reminds me of Coney Island. Most of the morning was spent delivering my goodies and drinking tea with appreciative hosts. I never even got to see the beautiful beach because I had to make a beeline for the bus.

The trip back was quite an experience. I managed to find the Central Bus Station, but I didn't stand in the right place, which involved me in a heated argument in Hebrew with a not-so-nice lady who claimed I had not been standing in line as long as she had, which wasn't so, so I stood my ground. Just as we got the matter straightened out amicably, a good-looking man behind her nudged me and asked in American-accented Hebrew if I had a sister named Ruth, a strictly American line. I answered emphatically, "NO" — it's hard to be coy in Hebrew — and we ended up sitting next to each other on the bus, where we discussed — believe or not — religion.

It turns out that he is a Baptist minister who set up a mission in Jerusalem and is doing very nicely converting Jews. The odd thing about these converts, as I understood him, is that they want to remain Jews and Zionists in all aspects except religiously — whatever that means. The objects of his attentions are mainly young people who are in what he calls a religious vacuum. It was a fascinating conversation and made the trip, which is normally about an hour and half, pass in no time.

We arrived in Jerusalem just after sundown and found that the bus service to my suburb had already been discontinued. Whereupon my gallant companion offered to take me home on something he called a motor-bike which was parked nearby. The winding rocky roads of Jerusalem are perilous enough in a bus but on this contraption I felt I was tempting fate. As he took the turns, I gripped his shoulders with all the adrenalin I could muster and prayed silently for safe arrival, consoling myself with the thought that, at worst, I would be perishing on holy soil. I got home thoroughly shaken up and decided next time to opt for cars. But when I thanked him for the ride I couldn't resist telling him: "Sorry, I'm not in a religious vacuum. I'm just brimming over with Jewish content."

Saturday is strictly a day of rest in Kiryat Moshe. No vehicles are permitted to drive within the community except for Arab buses which few patronize. It was a glorious sunny morning. I had no plans and no excuses, so I got into the spirit of the day, took a book and a chair out onto the big balcony intending to bask in the sun and read. I hadn't been there very long when several of my neighbors, whom I'd never seen before, appeared, apparently with the same idea in mind. We chatted for a while, then one question led to another and now they all know that I'm an "American" — an obvious curiosity as there are so few of us around. They spouted the usual clichés about Americans being spoiled and materialistic, a somewhat distorted view of us, probably gleaned from the movies. At first the conversation was friendly, then somehow, still in a light vein, it took a nasty turn.

"Why did you come? What are you doing here? What was wrong with America? No one expelled you." I couldn't believe what I was hearing. Then I got mad and took them on one by one and all together.

"Whose country do you think this is? The Turks', Britain's? *Eretz Yisrael* belongs to the entire Jewish people. I have as much right to be here as you. It's the natural place for a Jew to be — the one place in the world where commitment as a Zionist has some meaning. You criticize us Americans for not coming here, yet when we do, you suspect something must be wrong with us. Or else, why would we leave the fleshpots? Yes, we may be a little spoiled and materialistic. That should be our worst fault. The only shame is that there aren't more of us here because what we bring to this poor and backward land are valuable assets, not just cigarettes and instant coffee. We bring education, training, know-how, experience, organizational ability and a tradition of the democratic way of life."

I said a lot of other things, most of them unsettling, because, after that little speech, there was new respect and acceptance and the feeling that I am no longer an outsider. But none of us got to read any books that morning. Someone started to hum a tune and, before I knew it, I was swirled into a dance the likes of which I've never seen before. The dances from Palestine that I'm familiar with have the same names but that's where the comparison ends. No prancing, banging feet or jumping; instead the steps are a graceful glide that appear to be done on tip-toe.

*Later...*

I had lunch with the American gang and then went exploring the neighborhood with Dov Ben-Abba, a GI Harvard psychology man who was stationed in Cairo with the American Air Force during World War II and has an amazing knowledge of both Hebrew and Arabic. When I mentioned the balcony dialogue, he told me Americans are always on trial here. Since they keep expecting us to get fed up and leave, they are genuinely surprised if we stick it out. The two of us took a long hike through the surrounding area, past Jewish suburbs and the neighboring Arab villages out to the open fields. Backyards full of rocks, with only a lone stone-faced building jutting out here or there — stark stone and sunshine and a closeness to nature that makes you blink with awe.

On Saturday night, the chief recreation in Jerusalem is cinemas — movies to you — only tickets have to be ordered in advance. Nobody felt much like making the effort so a group of us went to town for coffee at the Atara Cafe, the students' hangout. Every cafe has its own clientele, like a favorite pub. We stocked up on *nasherei* and went home to listen to records.

So much for my first weekend in the Holy Land.

Love,
*Zippy*

*Jerusalem*

*October 30, 1947*

Dearest Mother, Dad and Naomi,

The Hebrew University held its official opening exercises yesterday morning. Donned my best duds and boarded the No. 9 bus to Mount Scopus, only to discover — admission by ticket or not at all. Very solemn and formal these official occasions. I managed to get the ticket but the doors closed promptly at 10:30, with me still outside. Missed most of the President's speech which I am told was very political — out on a limb for Arab-Jewish brotherhood. He was followed by the Rector, then everyone sang *Hatikvah* and shuffled out of the hall.

There is no official registration in the sense of signing up or arranging programs. It seems you just attend a chosen class and if you like it after hearing a couple of lectures, you ask the professor to sign a card which makes you eligible for credit. The University is still discussing arrangements for the special courses I selected; nothing moves very fast or efficiently in this country. So I have time to take off for some sightseeing.

Oh, I forgot to tell you about my tour to Gush Etzion. I went with GI Dov and Oded, a Sabra who lives in our student house and goes out of his way to bring the Americans closer to what he calls the real *Eretz Yisrael*. We set out at about 5:00 in the morning for town where we caught an Arab bus and headed for Hebron. The interesting thing about the tour was that each of the settlements we visited was progressively older than the previous one so we were able to see the patterns of development in kibbutzim and the way each added its own distinctive mark.

Our first stop was Kibbutz Revadim, which is only about four months old. Oded, who served as our guide, joined the settlement when it was established and was able to point out what had been accomplished in the two months since he had been there. There were two miserable huts serving as temporary living quarters; all the other physical amenities were equally makeshift. The only permanent fixtures were the security facilities — a barbed wire fence to designate the boundaries, a concrete water tower and sandbag barricades. In a word, their lifestyle was stark simple. The youngsters who had founded the settlement with Oded were from the non-religious Hashomer Hatzair movement.

After tramping a couple of miles over the hills of Judea, we arrived at a religious kibbutz, Ein Tzurim, which is about a year old. It already has a dining room that also serves as a synagogue, the beginnings of some industry, a leather tanning shed and a machine shop and, of course, cows and a chicken run. The kibbutzim in the hilly regions have less cultivable land and practically no sources of water so they must industrialize to some degree. Ein Tzurim is preparing for the rainy season with ingenuity. Trenches have been dug in a V-shape which slope down the hills, directing all rainwater to a central concrete drum, where the water is filtered for impurities and will serve as a year-round reservoir.

By 10:30 A.M. we were headed for Massuot Yitzhak, but instead of keeping to the road, which would have meant a hike of several miles, we took a shortcut over the mountains, literally mountain-climbed two huge steep hills which emptied into wadis. Looking up from the very bottom, all I could see was a ring of sky, marked by the radius of the mountain brim. Oded called our attention to the fact that one of these mountains had been the scene of an ancient Maccabean battle. Scrambling up the loose earth, holding my breath for fear of losing my balance, and scaling down the other side with the same cautious steps, I began to appreciate the heroism of those biblical warriors. Imagine running on foot or horseback-riding over that dangerous terrain, throwing stones or hurling spears as you went.

We came to two-year-old Massuot Yitzhak in time for lunch, which consisted of soup, stuffed peppers and clementina, a kind of tangerine. The first person we met there was a fellow student who showed us around. The houses were beautiful, surrounded by gardens and landscaped paths. In summer, the kibbutz members make a tidy sum by moving into tents and renting their houses to city vacationers. Vegetables had already been planted to make the kibbutz self-sufficient, to some extent.

About two miles further was our final stop, Kfar Etzion, which should be on your map because it is about four years old. A beautiful spot. Modern dining room, children's house, a real bathroom and shower house, culture hall and a fine library. They have a bee farm and furniture shop and a chicken run with the latest equipment. Very impressive. By now the pace has slowed down and every split second has ceased to be of urgency. Now they have time to talk, to point with pride to every little feature and to begin to enjoy life. The only problem is that they are smack in the heart of Arab territory so what sense of security can there be?

It was late and we were very tired but to get back to the bus we had to hike several more miles, using the shortest and hilliest route. To take our minds off our feet I suggested we play some old Girl Scout word games, which at least kept us alert. By the time we got back I was more tired than I can ever remember. But, now I had actually seen a kibbutz — in fact, four of them — a real eye-opener for a born and bred city girl.

Had a lovely time the other evening, strictly American Jewish bourgeois fun. Sidor Belarsky, the singer, was in Jerusalem for a one-night stand so Milt Schulman, a Chicago GI, and I and Morty C. and a friend double-dated. We had cocktails, a scrumptious dinner and deluxe seats at the theater. Belarsky was in great form. Had to wear low-heel shoes; my feet are still sore from that trek in the mountains.

Love,
*Zippy*

— NOTE ————————————————————

*Little did I know that only months later there would be fierce fighting in this area, that all these settlements would fall and almost all the men of Kfar Etzion would be massacred.*

22

*November 2, 1947*

Naomi Dear,

I received a very official-looking notice yesterday from the General Post Office advising me in very British jargon of the receipt of a postal packet which could be collected between the hours of 0800 and 1300 within a week of the notice if I do them the courtesy of opening it for postal inspection — graciously signed "Your Obedient Servant." Plus a P.S. stating that the Post Office is not open on Sundays in Jerusalem or Saturdays in Tel Aviv or on His Majesty's Birthday. Also, that one should never send guns, glue or checks through the mail.

In a typical American huff at all the formality, I presented myself at the Post Office, was duly frisked to my more than usual annoyance, and demanded to speak to whomever had signed himself my "Obedient Servant." My O.S. turned out to be a very debonair Arab with no sense of humor. After signing in two languages and showing my passport I was finally given the packet — which was only a letter, but bulky and very suspicious-looking. Asked to open it, I did so as slowly as possible while I watched my O.S. squirm. He looked so disappointed when all I drew forth was a stack of onionskin paper and some photos that I couldn't help commenting, "Maybe next time it'll be something you can confiscate." That did it. Roundly cursed in Arabic, I hurried to the nearest exit with my precious cargo in tow.

The delightful letter and photos were well worth the few bad moments, but I should tell you that the Post Office is in a perilous security zone, a predominantly Arab district where Jews are not particularly welcome. So don't punish me by sending bulky letters any more.

I think I have already answered most of your questions. For the rest, well, here goes:

*Film:* It is available. I haven't priced it but, like everything else, it's probably expensive. However, I haven't been doing much photographing for a number of reasons. Around the city, I feel like a tourist and look awfully silly snapping photos. On an outing, it is foolish to burden yourself with even the slightest excess baggage.

*Parcels:* I had to laugh when I heard that one of the students sent an SOS to America for food plus, of all things, shower curtains. The food eaten here is simply a different style and you either have to get accustomed to it or be glad you're losing weight. As for shower curtains, what this country needs is not so much shower curtains as a law against outhouses without toilet seats or sewage disposal. Mother Nature can cover up just so much before she protests by raising an awful stink.

But if you do want to send a food parcel some time, then indulge me with a can of tuna or salmon, pineapple or fruit salad. I am getting pretty tired of a steady diet of cucumbers, tomatoes, bread, jam and oranges every morning and evening and sometimes in between. But I'm not really complaining.

I haven't much experience with packages but friends are receiving them and paying through the teeth. Anyhow, don't send too much. Clothing should be washed or look worn; sometimes in Customs they get the notion that it's for resale and then you have to get an import license. It is unbelievable, but that's the way it is.

*Clothing:* I can also think of several other more important things you might like to pamper me with. Like some warm

24

clothing — maybe a dress, classic stuff: black, brown, wine or some other dull color. People are so conservative here. They stare at you sternly if you wear anything bright or colorful. Slacks seem to be confined strictly to the house; for school and the street they are taboo. I stick to a khaki twill skirt and simple blouses most of the time so as not to stand out in a crowd. I'm sure I'll never have the nerve to wear the lovely cotton dresses I brought when all the other girls are wearing only plain skirts, simple homemade dresses, never a girdle, and sensible shoes. Not that they are sloppy, just too too casual. Women go stockingless practically all the time except in winter when wool socks are the accepted thing. The sweaters worn here — some are beautifully made in intricate patterns — are more practical and attractive than those I brought. I think they must be hand knitted. Blouses are prettied up by hand embroidery, the first thing a girl is taught in school. I could have left home half the clothes I brought, but there is one item I should never have come without and that is a leather jacket. As for the boys, a hat or tie on any occasion is as way out as a monkey suit. Men wear knee-length khaki shorts to work, class, theater, concerts, cafes and to the best restaurants.

I've had bad luck with breakable items — sunglasses, wrist watch, even my typewriter; but radio, iron and travel clock are doing fine, all incidentally are the envy of the Palestinians. These "luxury" items give them the idea that every American is related to Rockefeller. They get this notion from the movies and from the way Americans come equipped for their comforts. Some brought even more stuff than I did: portable gramophones, furniture and Frigidaires.

The Palestinian students have only the bare necessities in their rooms. They envy us without admitting it and it comes out in the form of ridicule, some of it justifiable.

Anyone who is sensitive and doesn't want to be conspicuous, like me, just has to wear the dowdiest duds, things I wouldn't be seen dead in in New York.

Love,
*Zippy*

---

*Jerusalem*

*November 10, 1947*

Dear Everybody,

What magic in the mind makes it possible to be in the muddy depths of an ancient valley and have the illusion you are high on a windy hill? I wondered about it long after I returned to Jerusalem from my first tour of *Emek Yizre'el* (The Jezreel Valley). I went with Alizah, the daughter of your friend Professor Morris D. Levine of the Jewish Theological Seminary. We had no guide and no guidebook. But we had a map, sturdy shoes, backpacks and our American passports, the standard equipment for a *tiyul* (excursion). That, and a memorized list of practical travel talk.

It was a sunny day, the same kind of monotonous beauty that greets you every morning, the better part of 365 days. The idea of going on a *tiyul* developed over a cup of coffee. I said: "Why don't we go to Kibbutz Ginegar to visit my friends from Plugat Aliyah [young adult ZOA movement]?" And before we spotted the grinds at the bottom of the cup, the plan was underway.

At the Egged bus station, we purchased two tickets to Afula, despite advance warning that we might have to stand during the entire three-and-a-half-hour trip, penalty for not making reservations beforehand. With deliberate care, we wiped off our lipstick, mussed up our hair to give it that casual look, bought the latest edition of *Ha'aretz*, a Hebrew daily newspaper, and boarded the bus as inconspicuously as possible.

We were spotted though, not two minutes later, when Alizah turned to me and said: *"Eifo hacartisim?"* (where are the tickets?) in her big broad impossible accent. Now they knew we were Americans. People on the bus were disarmingly sociable, plaguing us with intimate questions while at the same time offering valuable, unsolicited information about the places we passed and the people who live there. They mentioned the names of their relatives in America — everybody has one — and were visibly disappointed when we couldn't claim acquaintance with them. When we finally reached Afula, we were flooded with invitations to visit them. And I'm sure they meant it.

From the bus stop, Afula looked like a sleepy little town that opens one eye when the buses come through and the other when the train passes. But in the fifteen-minute wait between buses, we discovered that it wasn't so. It turned out, in fact, that we were passing through one of the key cities in the *Emek*.

We'll never know whether it was instinct or good bus scheduling but we arrived at Kibbutz Ginegar at just the right time, 4:30 P.M., the end of the work day when everyone makes for the shower house to clean up and exchange news and gossip. My friends, spotting us from the distance, showered us with "Shaloms" and led us to a tent which was temporarily empty. That evening we had a long powwow with the gang — Nat Cohen, Rachel Wiener, Frieda and David Macarov, Miriam Rappaport, Ira Kahn, Hannah and Dov Popkin [Pelleg]. They were eager to get news about the movement and mutual friends in America and we wanted information about living on a kibbutz.

Breakfast in the States was always associated with black coffee and maybe toast, juice and eggs if you had time. In Jerusalem we had been initiated into the bread and salad routine. But Ginegar, noted for its good food, introduced us to a whole new gastronomic experience. The tables the next morning were laden with a mouth-watering variety of cheeses, herring, radishes, olives, *leben* (a mild yogurt) and honey. To work off the food, we set out on an extended sightseeing stroll around the *meshek* (the farm settlement). We were herded from barn, to chicken house, to children's house, to water tower, and our heads were crammed with statistics till twenty-five years of Ginegar were coming out of our ears.

Alizah, who was a dietitian in the WACs [the American Women's Army Corps], was fascinated by the kitchen and dining room, which were neat, clean and efficient-looking. I liked the water tower. It was the oddest shape I had ever seen, like a modern orange juice squeezer. Its base was shaped like a three-quarter oval from which jutted up a firm, flat slab that rose like an elevator shaft past the trees and the house tops. From it, one could see over the entire expanse of the *Emek*. Basically, it was a lookout post which was hooded by another oval protective shelf above. The inside of the base of the tower was used as a museum for the children and up the shaft was a winding spiral staircase.

From the lookout you could see clear over the Great Jezreel Plain to the haze of the hilltops across the Jordan River and back to where the hills of Gilboa collide with each other at ground level, seeming to crowd out the splash of rooftops and greenery that identify the surrounding settlements. Suddenly, in my mind's eye, the Plain became a colored canvas with predominant browns and greens and dashes of red, plough lines that pull from eye to sky, crossed only by intermittent ribbon-roads. The sun spattered the canvas with iridescent sunbeams that hopped about, conjuring up the song about the *Emek* being drunk and Mount Gilboa caressing Mount Tabor.

After a while the sun melted the canvas. That's when I noticed the Balfour Forest and the lovely swimming pool, which is actually a water reservoir. These were the physical features of Ginegar, but the real element, the people who live on the kibbutz, were still unfathomable. I watched our American *kvutzah* (group) at work with the other members of the kibbutz, at mealtimes and at leisure, and had the impression that, even though they were a foreign body, the transplant was beginning to take. Most of them were already fairly well-integrated. They couldn't tell me what it was like: "You have to live it to know it," they said. [All of them are still in Israel.]

Alizah and I each had an acquaintance or the name of a friend of a friend at settlements in the vicinity, so next day we set out for Bet Hashitah, our first stop. Our friend paraded us from fish pond to machine shop, from the knitwear factory to the beehives, past the plant nursery to the children's houses and finally to the dining room. The revived dehydrated potatoes and mock eggplant made us fondly remember the food at Ginegar. But on a loftier level, we listened raptly to the "you better believe it" Bible stories about Deborah the Judge and Barak waging war against Sisera and his forces. And practically across the "street" were the hills where Jonathan was killed and where King Saul fell upon his sword.

We had planned to go to other kibbutzim in the neighborhood, but the road curfew imposed by the British and effective after 6:00 P.M. was almost upon us, so we took to the highway. We reached our tent in Ginegar just seconds before somebody in heaven opened a trapdoor and let loose the wrath of the angels — the first winter rains. Our tent was not designed for this sort of conflict with nature. Torrents of water poured in, leaving us wet and cold. I developed a new respect for *chalutzim* (pioneers).

We caused a minor sensation that evening by tramping into the dining hall with our blue jeans rolled up to avoid trailing the cuffs in the mud. People nudged each other, pointed and stared. It seems that's not done, though the local girls wear shorts that are buttocks high and a lot more revealing. So why can't blue jeans be rolled up ? In a sense a kibbutz is a small town with defined and accepted attitudes toward insignificant things that are either done or not done, and woe unto American girls who wear yellow sweaters or argyle socks or their brother's shirts with the tails hanging out. The same conservative attitude doesn't apply to personal relationships, as I discovered that evening. A Sabra is a "he-man" with a very direct approach, reduced to YES or NO. After that, I learned not to flirt and even to be wary of smiling too broadly. Women are in very short supply in this country.

Next afternoon, there was a great deal of excitement in the air. Habimah, the national theater, had scheduled a performance of Ibsen's *Ghosts* at Gvat, one of the nearby kibbutzim, and Alizah and I were invited as guests of the Cultural Committee. Everybody piled into trucks, packed like sardines, and we plodded through the muddy roads to Gvat. I never knew I liked Ibsen so much until I saw it performed that evening. The audience was dressed for a baseball game. Not a drop of glamor but plenty of what theater is all about.

We had to leave the next morning and almost hated parting from our damp and dismal tent; we had grown attached to it.

Love,
*Zippy*

Naomi Dear,

It would be better to discuss the subject of your friend D. the *shaliach* (emissary) over a cup of coffee and not with an ocean between us. I gather he has been giving you very little room to maneuver your way out of your dilemma — to come or not to come.

I think I understand him much better now that I've been to kibbutzim and met other kibbutzniks. When he returns here he will have no choice but to return to his kibbutz; that's the way the system works. Economically, culturally, emotionally, socially, that's where his security is. And, if you think for an optimistic moment that you'll succeed in luring him elsewhere or trying to remake him to suit an image you've created, you may find it won't work. He is a true-blue kibbutznik, a rugged romanticist who is both realist and idealist, who has been disciplined, toughened, trained and indoctrinated in this mold from the outset.

Sure, he has plenty of freedom and independence in his personal behavior, in anything that doesn't relate to work assignments or obligations to the kibbutz. That is holy territory. For that, there is a rigid code, not unlike the silent vows the clergy take when they join an order. How this combination manages to make these guys uninhibited, inconsiderate of others and so super-confident, I haven't figured out. But they do have two shining qualities: loyalty and single-mindedness. So I doubt if you will get him to remain in the States. I don't know how you feel about him. All I can do is give you an idea of the type of life he will have to offer you here and I'm trying very hard to be objective in evaluating kibbutz life, not only for your sake, but in this case, and for very different reasons, for mine as well.

I've seen about ten kibbutzim since I've come, but even after three I could have begun to generalize, for the patterns are similar. But the patterns aren't all that counts. Physically they all look alike, more or less — resembling somehow the children's summer camps we know so well. Some have more land and more houses, others fewer houses or only tents, some have lush greenery and others are starkly bare, some have modern toilet facilities, others only outhouses; all of this depending on how long they have been on the land, on the ingenuity and industriousness of the members and on the natural resources of the kibbutz.

As I say, the pattern doesn't count so much. What seems to make for adjustment to kibbutz life is an attitude, a faith and belief that is absolutely part of you, that you don't stop to question or to think about. It is not only an ideal that is accepted intellectually or a rugged way of life that is learned physically; it is both of these and more. It also has to do with losing individualism to the extent that a man loses his independence when he marries or undertakes responsibilities that become so inextricably part of his life that he soon forgets what he forfeited in the first place. And I suppose, just as a mature man recognizes this quickly and enduringly, so the adjusted kibbutznik is the one who wholeheartedly accepts the role in society to which he married himself. He is free to divorce it at any time, but leaving a kibbutz is complicated, costly and socially ostracizing.

For Americans, the problem is more difficult. At Kibbutz Ginegar I observed and talked with our Zionist youth movement friends who live there. For the first couple of years the stress was on physical adjustment, training your body to do ten grueling hours of hard work a day, most of it monotonous, learning to forget whatever conveniences you were accustomed to consider as necessities; initially, the problem of learning to express yourself in another language and so on. The ones who are well-adjusted are those who have stamina and have ceased questioning their convictions.

It takes a forceful kind of courage that, until put to the test, you can't know you have. Unfortunately, the test is soul-wrenching and that's where the trouble is. Those whose bridges are burned behind them have no choice but to adjust, but Americans have a road back. It's tough to keep plodding through the mud in front of you when there's a paved highway behind you.

The kibbutz is self-contained, a complete life in a close-knit web, limited somewhat socially and a bit provincial, but it relieves you of the burdens, tensions and insecurities of organizing the economics of your life — no worry about where your next meal is coming from. The point to bear in mind is that kibbutzim are a historic necessity at this time, as much a challenge and maybe more so than the American pioneers faced. Your friend D. is right when he says that kibbutzim are the most important phenomenon in the country today and without them aspirations for a Jewish State are less meaningful. People in a city are just people in a city, living their own lives. In a kibbutz, it is all for one and one for all. And it comes down to asking yourself or me asking myself if we have the courage to adopt this lifestyle. Have we the tenacity and the patience to restrain our individuality, to cut ourselves to the cloth that everyone else is wearing, sustained only by the abiding conviction that you had a choice, made it and *this is it?*

Being a Zionist in New York is different from being one in *Eretz Yisrael* — not words, but deeds.

Well, that's about as realistic as I can paint it. And, if I don't sound persuasive one way or the other, it's because I am unpersuaded myself. If you want to be philosophical, I don't suppose it makes much difference in the totality of the universe whether you or I live here or there, in this society or that, as long as we make our mark by doing the best we can and believing in what we do. But the fact is that just by *being here* you count.

If I sound confused, I am. I am learning a different definition of Zionism and, in fact, a different definition of living in general.

Love,
*Zippy*

*Jerusalem*

*November 21, 1947*

Dear Everybody,

The University President, Dr. Judah Magnes, who is a former American, has invited the American students to an informal tea — I gather that there are about a hundred of us. Why anybody would want to drink tea at 10:30 in the morning unless they are sick is beyond me. I hope there'll be some coffee on hand too. Incidentally, Magnes has been here some twenty years and still speaks Hebrew with a pronounced American accent. Small comfort.

The special HU courses for overseas students have finally started: the guest lecturers are top-notch people. I'm having a hard time with the academic jargon — it's a whole new language. Until I learned the words for "social sciences" and "population," I couldn't even begin to follow the sociology lecture. So I'm doing a lot of word learning, reading or rather "studying" newspaper articles. The neighbor across the hall is an excellent teacher and has been helping out by grilling me in a weekly exam based on what I read. We leave the "exam" papers under each other's doors like a correspondence course.

The rest of the fellows on the floor try to get into the act by popping in to ask if I understand this or that word from whatever they happen to be reading. It's probably just an excuse to visit. They like having a woman around and kind of exploit me: a button that needs to be sewn or a shirt to be ironed in a hurry. I don't really mind. They are very attentive and shower me with little tokens of appreciation — flowers, cigarettes, etc., and loads of good company. In general, the students are serious and conscientious about studies, particularly the ones in this building who are either doing graduate work or finishing up their final year.

I've only been here about a month and already I'm a veteran explaining to new arrivals all the do's, don't dare do's and how to's — which may be of interest to you:

*Water*: Don't expect to find it on anybody's table. When traveling, use it only for rinsing out your mouth.

*Cold milk*: Obtainable, but hardly ever served. Although Tnuva milk is pasteurized and bottled, most milk isn't — it has to be boiled, then chilled. (Tnuva is a cooperative of the General Federation of Labor which distributes dairy food and other produce in its own stores and through local outlets.)

*Coffee*: Three quarters of a cup of boiled milk, a dash of coffee and, swimming on top, the "skin" that formed on the milk while it cooled. Or, alternatively, Turkish Coffee. Also something called *botz*, which means "mud," and that's exactly what it looks and tastes like.

*Restaurants*: Places where you have to eat when nobody invites you for a home-cooked meal. There are two types of restaurants, those that are exclusively dairy (some belong to Tnuva) and others where meat is also served. The most popular of these is the *Mitbach Hapoalim.*

Have to stop now . . .

Love,
*Zippy*

*Jerusalem*

*November 24, 1947*

Naomi Dear,

I must tell you about some of my neighbors. Typecasting isn't fair but the native-born Palestinian Jews, called Sabras, literally a cactus that it prickly on the outside but has a firm sweet fleshy inside, are a new breed. Try this concoction: rugged and unpolished, unsophisticated, uninhibited, often shy, uncomplicated, direct, gentle, ruthless, undaunted, self-reliant, with a gift for improvisation.

One of them, Ami, lives next door, a big strappping guy who majors in Zoology and already looks very much like a zoo keeper. He hides a very handsome face under a golf cap and, when people are looking his way, pretends to be embarrassed. He has the typical Palestinian slouch. It consists of sitting with one shoulder completely relaxed and the other way up in the air, one arm limping over a knee, posed to mimic "Le Penseur" and supposed to convey an air of ease and urbanity. Actually, it is the best position for a lurching pounce or a quick retreat. He also has a disarming smile that he flashes in odd moments, provoked by nothing in particular.

Across the hall is another Sabra, the mild but devastating type. Formerly President of the Students'

Organization, he is reputed to be brilliant. Last night we had a special *kumsitz* (a kind of powwow, with or without a campfire) in his honor. He just received his M.A. and came running in, proud and excited, looking for someone to celebrate with. So in honor of the occasion we had not only tea but tea with SUGAR. He rooms with a chemistry major, a Tel Aviv hobo who plays the violin passionately and purposely unbuttons the third button of his shirt so that the hair on his chest will show. He's a research student. That means he sits in his room and thinks instead of going to classes. He once told me what his research topic was and when I looked unimpressed he was mortally offended and proceeded to inform me that he was one of the few people in the world working on this topic. That, I could believe.

One room is empty pending new arrivals this week. It was formerly occupied by a Brazilian flautist who spoke Hebrew with a German accent. His roommate was Oded, my *tiyul* companion who even though he too has moved away still comes to see me religiously twice a week. He literally *sees* me, sits and stares — a Palestinian pastime. I remind him of a cousin in America whom he has never seen but with whom he carries on a heated correspondence. So we talk about the things that they correspond about.

Downstairs are some normal people: an American couple, two local couples and two American GI singles, Morty Rubin and Sam Bloom, whom I mother, sister and so forth. They are grand kids and share with me a yearning for hot water, steam heat and broiled lamb chops. We invite each other to supper and hometown small talk every Saturday night and drool over old magazines.

Down the road apiece, but not so far as to prevent me from frequent drop-ins whenever I feel like it, is the American ghetto, Pension Pax, the most comfortable and most expensive of all the student houses. Meals can be had there but at a price that makes you prefer the twenty-minute trip to town. On Saturdays, the landlady takes advantage and charges twenty-two *grush* (about a dollar) for the same meal we pay twenty for on weekdays, simply because there are no buses and it is a question of either her food or your bread and jam. I don't mind the price but the food is greasy and the talk is always in English. I do eat there sometimes on Friday nights because the Shabbat atmosphere is very nice.

The local boys I've met don't go in much for anything "Jewish" — they are too busy being Jews in the bigger sense, I guess.

The weather is cockeyed. One day, bright and sunny. Next day, bitter cold and rain — and sometimes the same combination on the same day just to confuse the enemy.

*Zippy*

---

— NOTE

*Up until now, concerned mainly with studies, seeing the country and getting to know the local scene, I was blithely unaware of the double life most of my fellow students were leading. They were being secretly trained by the Haganah — under the very noses of the British — laying the foundation for an independent Jewish defense organization.*

*Raised in a Zionist home in America, my yearning for Jewish sovereignty had focused on youth movement meetings and activities. The Haganah, on the other hand, were already putting into practice the Zionist dream of asserting Jewish national identity in Palestine. It wasn't long before I joined them.*

*But never in my wildest dreams did I imagine that the possibility of a Jewish State would soon become a reality and that my student days would be short-lived.*

## Part Two

# A Never-to-be-Forgotten Night

*THE TWENTY-NINTH OF NOVEMBER*

*After almost thirty years of Mandatory rule in Palestine, the British, no longer able to cope and faced with mounting world pressure, turned over to the United Nations the problem of conflicting Jewish and Arab national claims and aspirations.*

*The UN appointed UNSCOP (United Nations Special Committee on Palestine) to find a solution. Their recommendation was to partition Palestine into two states, an Arab state and a Jewish state, with special international status accorded to Jerusalem.*

*November 29, 1947 was the red-letter day, the day the UN General Assembly, sitting at its headquarters in Flushing Meadows, New York, voted to approve UNSCOP's recommendations, thus heralding the end of the British Mandate.*

*Would the British really leave? What would happen afterwards? Although the Jewish community accepted the compromise, the Arabs refused to accept even the idea of a Jewish State. The Partition Plan, as it was called, now had international sanction, but there was no authority to implement it. So, in effect, it created new chaos and confusion which eventually erupted into war. The mighty Arab states surrounding Palestine joined forces to prevent a Jewish State from coming into being. They almost succeeded.*

*But, for the Jewish people throughout the world and especially for the 600,000 Jews who lived in Palestine at that time, the UN resolution meant the creation of a previously promised and dearly yearned-for Jewish*

*National Home and the fulfillment of a two-thousand-year-old dream. Not just a dream, but also a desperately needed haven for the remnant of European Jewry who had survived the German death camps. A chance to create a sovereign Jewish State in which to build a strong, self-reliant society so that no Holocaust would ever again annihilate the Jewish people. That, after all, was what Zionism was all about.*

*Jerusalem went wild with joy the day the UN voted approval of the Partition Plan. And wonder of wonders, I was where it was all happening!*

Dearest Mother, Dad and Naomi,

I walked in a semi-daze through the crowds of happy faces, through the deafening singing of *"David, Melech Yisrael, chai, chai vekayam"* (David, King of Israel, lives and is alive), past the British tanks and jeeps piled high with pyramids of flag-waving, cheering children. I dodged motorcycles, wagons, cars and trucks which were racing madly up and down King George V Street, missing each other miraculously, their running boards and headlights overflowing with layer upon layer of elated, happy people. I pushed my way past the crying, kissing, tumultuous crowds and the exultant shouts of "Mazal tov" and came back to the quiet of my room . . . to try to share with you this never-to-be-forgotten night.

The light in my room was still on from last night. I had planned to go to sleep early since rumor had it that voting at the UN on the Partition Plan would probably be postponed for another day. But, at about 11:00 P.M. there was a knock on the door: "We're getting through to America. Come on down. The voting's tonight." Ten pajama-clad bodies crowded into a room with space enough for five and sat tensely around the battered radio for what seemed like hours while vain attempts were made to get clear reception from Lake Success. We got through just as the announcement of the majority vote was made: thirty-three in favor, thirteen against and ten abstentions.

Ecstatic, we hugged and kissed each other frantically, then stood rigidly at attention and sang *Hatikvah* fervently. Out came bottles of wine, biscuits and candy. We ate and drank and held a solemn little ceremony, then dashed to our rooms, hurriedly slipped on whatever clothing was on hand and banged on all the doors to wake up those who had slept through the good news. All the students in the building scrambled up to the roof and, under the warmth of moonglow and wine, danced deliriously. Then we made a snake line to the nearest houses, banging on the shutters and doors, shouting the news as we went. In a seemingly endless column, we wound our way to the next community, Bet Hakerem, where the Teachers Seminary is and where most of its students live. The streets were already full, ring upon ring of dancing groups circling in a frenzied hora. Ours was the last and largest circle.

Arms linked, marching six abreast, singing all the way, the battalion of students advanced, shouting the news to neighbors who poked their sleepy heads out of windows and doors to see what the commotion was about, straight to Hamekasher, the bus terminal. Confronting the watchman with the news, we demanded a bus to take us to town. He was so excited he provided three. In a mad scramble we piled in, body on body; down the road we raced like a million hearts on fire, headed for the heart of Jerusalem.

The streets in the city were beginning to fill as the news got around. People poured out of their homes in a continuous ever thickening stream. In the center of town crowds of happy people, hugging each other, dancing horas and jigs, headed spontaneously, as we were headed — drawn by some magnetic force — to the courtyard of the fortress-like Sochnut (Jewish Agency) building, which for years housed the hopes for a Jewish State in Palestine. Out came a flag and onto the balcony came Golda Myerson [Meir]. There were no words to suit the moment. Choked with emotion, she managed to say "Mazal tov," and down came tears, oceans of unrestrained happy tears. All night streams of joyful crowds assembled in the courtyard milling in and out — to pay homage, to give vent to exultant feelings that welled up from deep inside.

A group of us marched to the press room of the *Palestine Post* to get the latest news from Morty and Dov, our friends who work there. Another round of drinks and embraces and crazy dances while we waited for the historic First Edition to come off the presses. At 4:30 in the morning, flushed with excitement, ignoring the wet ink, we passed our copies around for everyone to autograph, including an English Tommy who wandered in for a drink. Then Morty, Dov, Milt, and Ray Sussman, and I and several student friends who had come with me headed back to the Sochnut building, just in time to see a streak of warm beauty spring up out of the horizon and smile good morning to us. We looked at each other, drew closer together, wrapped arms about each other's chilled shoulders and felt the thrill of experiencing a historic wonder, dawn bidding Shalom to a Jewish State.

Our group consisted of about fourteen fellows and a few girls, from about as many countries. We made our way singing to Morty's room, not far away, where we found the landlord so elated he didn't know what to do for us first. Ever the practical person, I suggested food and prepared sandwiches, fruit and coffee while we drank yet another "*Lechaim.*" Leaving the house, we were met by scores of morning crowds, some from the night before, some fresh out of bed, kissing and embracing and shouting "Mazal tov!" And as we rounded the corner into Keren Kayemet Street, where the Sochnut is, whiz came the motorcycles, lorries, cars and the children, now awake, and took up the gaiety where we had left off. Spontaneous parades formed, led by a flag bearer and a couple of drunken British soldiers — this time, thank goodness, unarmed.

The sun was getting warmer and warmer, a glorious day. The end of November, and seventy-five degrees of heartwarming sunshine was bearing down on a happy city. The foreign correspondents and Pathé men were on the job photographing the British tanks which were suddenly converted into flying transport for anyone who could climb aboard, sing, shout and wave a flag. We joined the crowds, going from one end of King George V Street to the other, meeting friends and fraternizing with the English soldiers, who were as happy as we were about the end of tension and ill feeling between us. All they wanted was to go home. With each round we ended up at the Sochnut again; every crowd did.

Rumor had it that Ben-Gurion had just arrived from Tel Aviv and would make a personal appearance. Sure enough, there he was, standing on the balcony of the Sochnut building. He looked slowly and solemnly around him — to the rooftops crammed with people, to the throngs that stood solid in the courtyard below him. He raised his hand. An utter silence waited for his words: *"Ashreynu shezachinu layom hazeh."* (Blessed are we who have been privileged to witness this day.) He concluded with *"Techi Hamedinah Ha'ivrit"* (Long Live the Jewish State — it doesn't have a name yet) and called for *Hatikvah*. A solemn chant rose from all sides. The moment was too big for our feelings. There were few dry eyes and few steady voices. Ben-Gurion tossed his head back proudly, tenderly touched the flag that hung from the railing and charged the air with electricity when he shouted defiantly, "WE ARE A FREE PEOPLE."

How I wished you could have heard his words and been here for this memorable night and never-to-be-forgotten morning. It was too unbelievable.

Making my way to the bus to go home for a camera and a wash, I noticed that all the cafes and wine shops had flung open their doors — drinks on the house. Flags were hoisted everywhere and shopkeepers had decorated their windows with photos of Theodor Herzl, whose words have inspired and sustained Zionists until this day: "If you will it, it is no dream." Now that it was happening, it seemed more than ever like a dream. My heart was bursting from joy.

*Later that night . . .*

I grabbed my camera, changed clothes and joined my friends to return to the city and the excitement. Notices were already prominently displayed announcing a mass meeting to be held in the Sochnut courtyard at 3:00 in the afternoon, and a very impressive affair it was. We had already heard that there were incidents of Arab ambushes on the road from Haifa to Jerusalem. The crowds were more sober and, when told to, dispersed in an orderly and disciplined manner, everyone going to his own home and his own family celebration. We had ours too, then a hot bath and off to sleep, trying to make up for about fifty non-stop hours of delirium.

Your loving daughter,
*Zippy*

*Jerusalem*

*December 4, 1947*

Dearest All,

The morning after the great day was quiet and everydayish, except that flags still hung from every balcony and people in the street, though still jubilant, were solemn and uncommunicative. There were reports of more Arab ambushes of Jewish buses on the Haifa-Jerusalem road near Lydda airport and more to be expected. Also Arab strikes, a potentially dangerous situation.

Precautions are being taken. Evening classes at the University are being curtailed, as the buses have to pass through the Arab sector of the city. In addition, the students in our building are being organized to do guard duty to protect us in the event of attack from the neighboring Arab villages. We are told that the local police and Home Guard units are well-prepared and ready for anything.

I don't know what that means but the feeling is that not too much will be going on, probably only sporadic incidents or, at most, the kind of thing we've had thus far — ambushes, stray shots and stone throwing. At the moment, the Arabs are still unorganized. All I can tell you is NOT TO WORRY. The one thing I can do without right now is frantic letters from home. So please be sensible parents and live up to the wonderful reputation I have given you, telling everyone how you encouraged me to come and how pleased and proud you are that I am here at this time.

In answer to your questions about how the climate and the setup here would suit you if you were to come for a visit or to stay, I don't think I can answer until I have been here longer and know the country better. All I can say is that with all the uncertainties and insecurity of life in this country, one constant is clear: this is the place for Jews to be, especially those who consider themselves Zionists. Zionism in America can mean only one thing now, what it really implied in the first place, *Aliyah* (immigration). What else can there be? Somebody has to help make the Jewish State a reality. What a decade to be living in. And what a future to be part of!

I wish I had time to continue . . . but I don't.

Love,
*Zippy*

*December 7, 1947*

Dearest Folks,

From your end of the ocean or ours, it is still a holiday of sorts. The date rings a bell . . . Pearl Harbor, the trigger for American entry into World War II. I try not to think about that — about anything that has to do with war.

I am sitting in my room looking mournfully at a lovely ceramic menorah and watching two little candles dwindle into their sockets. It is the second day of Hanukkah, the Feast of Lights, but you wouldn't know it because the streets are dark, all public ceremonies have been cancelled and all the local students have been mobilized.

It's vacation time at the University and, though I would love to see more of the country, it isn't wise to travel around right now, so I am staying put. I'm also unable to pick up mail for a week or so. The trip to Mount Scopus is not the safest in the world and there are days one cannot go up for lack of a convoy. I suggest you start addressing my mail c/o Pension Pax, New Montefiore, Jerusalem.

I have no idea what the American papers are feeding you about the situation here. Arab attacks are gathering momentum and forcing the Jewish community to organize resistance to protect itself. Censorship prevents me from going into details.

Things seem to be surprisingly well under control, the only time they get out of hand is when the Goddamn British stick their noses in. Everybody here thinks we could handle the situation effectively if only the British would stay out of it or stay neutral.

The morale of the Jewish community in Palestine is fantastic. Unity and purposefulness pervade everything —

every single person is caught up in the needs of the hour. I can tell you I wouldn't have missed this experience for a lifetime of illusions about Zionism and Palestine lived in the "quiet" of New York. You are part of a struggle that is bigger than your own individual striving for self-attainment and self-preservation. There is an overpowering sense of belonging, of being needed and of being wanted. A commitment you cannot reject.

Living here at this time you learn the art of taking care of yourself, of being cautious where caution can be a matter of life and death, of being constantly alert. Thank goodness, I have grasped the essentials quickly. There are times when it pays to be an apt pupil in other than academic matters.

Can you imagine this: the door just opened and a shy sweet neighbor stuck in his hand, not his head, clutching two little posies of wild flowers that he had collected on the way home from work to cheer up us "foreigners" far away from home at holiday time. These guys are really taking good care of us.

I'll try hard not to neglect you but make allowances because I am getting very busy.

Love,
*Zippy*

— NOTE ——————————————————————

*What I was "getting very busy" with — it can now be told — was joining the Haganah, the underground Jewish defense organization. The next letter, describing the induction ceremony, was written much later and, to evade the censor, taken to the States by one of the returning students.*

*December 1947*

Dear Mother, Dad and Naomi,

I guess you've been in the dark long enough. But, PLEASE, don't share this letter with anyone. It's only for your information.

While I was sitting one day in a student hangout, Cafe Brazil, someone I didn't know passed me a note setting a mysterious appointment with another unknown party, who asked if I would do my share to help defend Jerusalem. With typical impulsiveness I said "Yes," never realizing what I was letting myself in for. The swearing-in ceremony was in the best cloak-and-dagger tradition and very impressive. A dark room in the basement of the Rehaviah High School, with only a dim light shining on a table draped with a Jewish flag. Sitting behind the table were three men, their faces hidden in the shadows, who questioned me carefully. Then, confronted with a Bible and a pistol, I was sworn in: a simple, powerful, pertinent pledge. Only a select group had been chosen, those whose background, loyalties and attitudes had been quietly investigated, and I was proud to have passed muster.

For convenience sake, the American girls were put into a special unit and assigned a group leader who didn't understand, or refused to speak, a word of English. Presto, we were part of an illegal army, the most unsoldier-like soldiers ever seen. The nearest any of us had ever gotten to firearms was at a shooting gallery. Lipstick and toilet paper were our true heritage. In a way, the full seriousness of our act didn't really register for a while. That day, we saw only the funny side of it and giggled all the way home.

Our first assignment, as I look back on it, was real kindergarten play but we were so convinced of its importance that we took it in dead earnest. Our instructions were to guard the house we lived in, two persons to a shift, twice a week, patrolling the grounds and the roof of the building . . .

—————— — *NOTE* ——————————————————————————

*A few years ago, while rummaging though some old papers, I made an unexpected and fantastic find, a document dated December 1947, detailing instructions for guard duty. I guess my Haganah commander had asked me to translate it and make sure that all the American students clearly understood what they were supposed to do.*

INSTRUCTIONS FOR GUARD DUTY
(Translation for American students)
Read, sign and return to Z. Borowsky

According to information we have received there is a possibility of an Arab attack in our neighborhood and of house searches for arms by the (British) Army and Police.

THE PURPOSE OF THIS NOTICE IS TO:

1) Advise guards and tenants of their assignments in the event of such an attack or house search.
2) Prevent panic and confusion.
3) Lessen the chances of endangering the tenants or the confiscation of arms because of lack of instruction.

Please Note that these instructions are NOT A ROUTINE NOTICE but specific guidelines in view of the general situation.

Remember that in most cases where accidents occurred during Guard Duty they were due to a CARELESS ATTITUDE regarding the instructions or CARELESSNESS IN THE CARRYING OF ARMS.

## GENERAL INSTRUCTIONS

All tenants in the building are requested to see that the main door is kept locked day and night in order to prevent surprise attacks and surprise searches.

Remember that both the British Army and Police headquarters have formally issued instructions NOT to make house searches. Any search made is being done without orders from above and in order to annoy or provoke. Therefore, in the event of an attempt to search the house or to surround the building, do the following:

1) See that the main door is closed.
2) Do not open the door under any circumstances.
3) Explain to the would-be searchers that you are aware of the standing orders that no searches are to be made.
4) Do not answer any questions pertaining to tenants, responsible people, location of keys, etc.
5) Assemble a crowd to help prevent the search from being carried out.

## INSTRUCTIONS TO GUARDS

1) Be on the alert for any activity in the vicinity of the building.
2) Every guard is responsible for the arms entrusted to him and should report to the guard who relieves him about the ammunition supplies and whatever took place during the shift.

## ORGANIZATION OF DUTY ROSTER

1) For the present, Guard Duty will be organized into three shifts:

> 5:00 P.M. - 9:00 P.M.
> 9:00 P.M. - 1:00 A.M.
> 1:00 A.M. - 5:00 A.M.

2) Every shift will receive arms and ammunition and/or specific instructions from the previous shift or from the person in charge.

3) The last shift will be responsible for returning the arms to the appointed place.

4) If a Police patrol should appear in the vicinity at the time the last shift ends the person in charge should be contacted before the arms are returned to the appointed place.

5) Guards are requested not to smoke or converse in loud tones while on duty.

6) Be careful not to publicize the fact that the building is being guarded.

7) If it is necessary to contact the person in charge or to alert the next shift, then ONLY ONE of the guards is to leave his post to arrange the matter.

8) Contact the person in charge:

   a) If suspicious persons are lurking in the vicinity and cannot provide satisfactory explanations for their presence when asked to identify themselves.

   b) When an Army or Police patrol indicates an intention to search or surround the building.

## OPEN FIRE ONLY

1) If fired upon by attackers and you are able to determine the direction from which they came or their position. (Remember that there is adequate guard coverage in Montefiore and Givat

Shaul and indiscriminate fire may cause casualties to our own people.)

2) When you perceive without doubt a group of ARMED ARABS endeavoring to infiltrate the vicinity and they do not respond to the command halt.

DO NOT OPEN FIRE

1) Even when fired upon by Police or Army personnel - immediately leave the roof and inform the person in charge.

2) On any of the buildings in the vicinity.

INSTRUCTIONS TO TENANTS (IN THE EVENT OF ATTACK OR SHOOTING)

1) Turn off all the electricity. Open the windows (to prevent breakage of glass and subsequent accidents), close the shutters and lock all external doors and shutters (in the order indicated).

2) Do not stand near windows or doors. Lie flat on the bed.

3) Stay in your room unless instructed to the contrary.

1. Elijah Lewie
2. Martha Beerman
3.
4. Bill Yaron
5. Al Yanov
6.
7.
8.
9.
10.

11.
12. David
13.
14.
15.
16.
17.
18.
19.
20.

Dearest All of You,

That box of goodies you were good enough to send will just have to rot in its wrappings in Kibbutz Ginegar, because that's where it landed with one of the new arrivals. The situation is such that nobody has the right to endanger a friend in order to collect a parcel and send it on to me. Nor do I relish the risk of a bus ride to the kibbutz to get it. No parcel could be worth the danger of being ambushed in the hotbed of activity on the Jerusalem-Tel Aviv road. Every curve, clump of trees, cluster of rocks or mound of earth provides cover for Arab snipers. The roads have become the most dangerous place in the country.

The University held its graduation ceremony the other day. I couldn't go, but Dov covered it for the *Post* and told me that, for a change, it was very informal, exceedingly dull, and unimpressive. So to hell with degrees. But the refreshments were good. The problem is that it's hard to get enthused over a normal activity when everything around you is so abnormal.

There are constant interruptions as I write this. The last was a blackout for over an hour. These student houses have the lousiest electrical connections. There are five Physics majors in the building and they prolong the blackout by arguing among themselves about which wire theoretically is on the blink and how it should have been connected in the first place, while we poor Humanities students wait for them to link us back onto the network.

Another interruption was the arrival home of some of our boys from one of their mysterious missions. To celebrate their safe return we opened a dusty bottle of Carmel Port, the last of the reserves. I got my first and only Hanukkah present, a wonderful penknife, given to me by Ami, who personally scratched an inscription on it and assured me that he has had it through many bad moments. It has more gadgets on it than I know how to use, but the corkscrew is the one that came in handy. Like everything in Palestine, it is kind of rough in appearance, but the blades are stainless steel and kept dangerously sharp.

School is starting again in a few days at the end of Hanukkah vacation but I hardly think classes will take place as scheduled because most of the students are too busy with Haganah and defense activites to attend, and the same goes for the instructors, professors and administrative staff.

Things really are perking up now. Hardly a day passes without some incident rocking the bottom out of you. But don't take the foreign correspondents' reports too seriously; after all they are paid to find exciting and sensational news. Here's an example of what I mean: the *Post* just printed two stories, wired to America by foreign correspondents — one by Carter Davidson and the other by an equally well-known writer — and ran them full length, along with a local reporter's account of the same incident. What the foreign correspondents had written were clearly gross exaggerations and far off the mark. What had actually happened was common knowledge to everyone here.

Please give my address to the world since there is so little mail from you. I crave for letters with news from home, or maybe just to know that people give a good Goddamn about what is happening at this end of the world.

Had to laugh when I heard that American Zionists were "grooming themselves" for political posts in the upcoming State. Here everyone is more concerned with attaining and securing the State.

*Zippy*

*December 17, 1947*

Dear All,

The room was so cold I could hardly grip the pen firmly. Need to conserve kerosene. Had to stop, light the stove, drink a cup of hot tea and am now trying to type.

The two-hour class scheduled for this morning was cancelled because the instructor who commutes from Haifa didn't want to tempt fate on the dangerous roads, for which I don't blame him. Since he won't be showing up, I'll forgo the trip to Mount Scopus to ask in vain if there is mail for me.

The University has finally succumbed to the will of the students and the needs of the community and arranged a schedule more in line with the realities of the situation. Students have been divided into two groups, Natural Sciences and Humanities, and each faculty will alternate with two weeks of classes and then two weeks "free." This will enable us to continue studies with a minimum of interruption and, at the same time, free students and faculty to continue the other activities everyone is engaged in, also without too much interference.

Getting to the campus is no simple matter. The buses to Mount Scopus are constantly being harassed as they pass through the Arab communities en route. They have to climb a torturously winding road and are a vulnerable target for ambush at every curve. I heard from those who went to school this morning that the Hadassah ladies are arranging funds for armored buses for transport to and from the hospital compound, which will also serve the University campus. The armored buses will really be only regular buses which will be covered with two outer sheets of thick steel in order to give at least some protection against snipers. Nothing short of a blitzkrieg can hurt us now.

The bad news is that my roommate has been very unwell during the past month. It's been one helluva time, not only for her but for all those around her. I guess I better do some explaining. I thought it was the heightened tension in the city that had gotten to her. But apparently, she arrived here with some personal difficulties because, from the beginning, she was under treatment by a psychoanalyst. I knew nothing of this, only that I sensed she was removing herself further and further from things actual to things internal, until an emotional combustion occurred that floored me. I had underestimated the seriousness of the symptoms. I thought it was just moods, bad temper or homesickness, combined with fear of the security situation here. So I showered her with large doses of sympathy, understanding and concern, mothering and reassuring her till I was worn out with the effort. Finally, she became violent and clearly unable to control herself and I was at a loss to know whom to turn to.

I did some sleuthing — followed her one day — and discovered that there was a doctor in the picture. I got his name and had a long talk with him. It seems the case was infinitely more complicated and serious than I had supposed or even dreamed of. The doctor, who is a well-known figure in Jerusalem and regularly deals with children brought to Palestine as Youth Aliyah wards, recommended treatment which is not available except in England or America. Her father in England was called long distance and flew over within a few days. So it became my job to get her to go with her father without duress and, at the same time, without giving her any indication of what was wrong. It was a very tough job, but they finally left yesterday by plane. Even up to the last minute it was hectic, as I had to pack her things in less than an hour.

Aside from interrupting my studies, work and personal peace of mind, it was an overwhelming responsibility simply because she leaned so heavily on me for support and trusted no one else.

My first reaction to the new, all-dimensional freedom was to remove the empty bed in the room and discourage all hopeful roommates. I need some privacy for a week to recuperate. I even went to the extreme extravagance of going to a beauty parlor to have my hair washed, to feel and look like a human being again. In any case, it was too cold in the room to wash it at home.

This should hold you for a while.

Love,
*Zippy*

*Jerusalem*

*December 20, 1947*

Naomi Dear,

My next door neighbor, Ami, was in great form this morning and fixed breakfast for me, topped off by delicious hot cocoa and an American cigarette, bummed from somebody else for the occasion. The fact that it was the cheapest brand available, Rum and Maple, didn't detract from the quality of the intention.

This guy is your typical Sabra, but a type all his own. As natural as nature itself and equally unpredictable. When he is at home, which isn't often these days, what with his "hush-hush" activities, he gets up at about 7:00 in the morning, bangs on the wall between our rooms and shatters the quiet with a resounding Tarzan call "Tzippeeeeeee!" The reason he has to wake me up is because he has usually borrowed my alarm clock to get up in the middle of the night to go off on a mission, which I am sworn not to question him about. If he doesn't hear me answering immediately or moving about — the walls are paper thin — then all six feet of him shuffle into the hall and he bangs on the door loud enough to wake the dead. That, or he pokes his head around our mutual balcony and serenades me with more Tarzan stuff.

The routine has only just begun. He then starts shaving, a ceremony in itself, taking half an hour to smear his entire face with soap lather — ears, lips and neck included — and to remove it; once with the grain, once against it. Much splashing around in water, which is COLD, while I am patiently waiting my turn to get into the washroom.

When he considers himself ready for inspection, he bangs on the door again, sticks his head in and grins from ear to ear. I ask you, can you be angry at a guy like that? He also draws exceedingly well, really very talented, and often leaves sketches under the door for my approval. Some of them are rather suggestive, but perhaps that's just my suspicious nature. He has taken a great shine to me and doesn't bother to hide it, and talks about me to whomever will listen, giving me such a buildup that I cringe with embarrassment.

He speaks a flawless English, which is a problem. So we have agreed that everyday conversations will be strictly in Hebrew but "profound" discussions on religion, Palestine, politics and the human condition will be partly in English, so that I don't trip over my tongue.

Have to stop, but thought this would amuse you. Unfortunately, there is very little these days that is amusing. The euphoria of last month has evaporated. It is clear that no one is going to hand the Jewish State to us on a silver platter, certainly not the British. We'll have to fight for it. More I can't say.

Love,
*Zippy*

On the sun deck of the *Marine Jumper* en route to British Mandatory Palestine. Left to right: Carmi Charney, Dov Ben-Abba, the author, and other students.

Identity card issued by the British Mandatory Government of Palestine.

Former Vice-President Henry A. Wallace (second from right)
sharing a joke with a group of American students at the Hebrew
University (*Photo Ilani*).

Left to right: Dov Ben-Abba, the author, Mordechai Chertoff and Ray
(Sussman) Noam in Jerusalem on November 30, 1947, holding news-
papers announcing the UN vote on the Partition Plan for the creation
of a Jewish State (*courtesy of Ray Noam*).

# Part Three
# The "POP" of the Popcorn

Dear Everybody,

It gets so confusing trying to negate what you are and what you were conditioned to and at the same time trying to be an integral part of where you are — a totally new and different set of circumstances.

Christmas Eve, for example, a group of us American students were out walking in the rain — not by choice — and somebody started humming "Jingle Bells." We all howled with laughter: it was so completely out of tune with what we were doing — guard duty in the backwoods of Jerusalem.

The fact is that the Jews in Palestine are fighting an *undeclared war* with both the British and the Arabs. Everyone is expected to share in security measures to help protect the community. We all do guard duty and, in addition, I have joined a first aid course.

We are literally at the front lines and whatever we do is for real. We actually get to *see* more of the news than ever hits the headlines. What is reported back to you is the "pop" of the popcorn — the part that makes the most noise but gives no hint at all of the flavor. The atmosphere in Jerusalem is charged with tension, though outwardly calm, and nothing in sight to relieve it. I just looked around the room in a useless search for what to write about to somehow convey to you what is going on.

Perched on my bed is Carmi, batting his brains out writing book reviews for the *Post*; in a corner of the room is Alizah, knitting placidly while glued to the Forces Broadcast. Staring out into space is my introspective Sabra neighbor, Miriam. Morty R. is huddled in the far corner reading and I am typing like mad. We seem to be unaware of each other, yet every few minutes one of us comments on the shooting: its distance, direction, what sort of weapons, etc., as if we were discussing the latest movie or a change in the weather.

The first time you hear a royal volley your heart flips to attention. But after a while you get used to it. Sometimes it becomes a guessing game: Who is shooting at whom? If it's pot shots, generally it is the Arabs at us. If it's indiscriminate fire, it's bound to be the British. And when it is a one-time good-sized *zetz*, that's us. The night magnifies the sounds, especially in the open country. When you hear gunfire from miles away, it tends to sound like it's right in your backyard. You get so used to it, it makes you nervous when it is too quiet.

At night your iron shutters are pulled down tight, and you know your friends are standing guard so you can go to sleep and have sweet dreams about American ice cream sodas and tile bathrooms with hot and cold running water — the ideal Jewish State.

Not to worry; it'll be o.k.

Love,
*Zippy*

*Jerusalem*

*December 29, 1947*

Naomi Dear,

Living with people ain't easy. This evening I had to participate in a committee meeting consisting of all the girls in the building. With my roommate gone, the countdown is now five girls who are supposed to share rooms, but actually each of us has a separate room, with the exception of two who are sharing a room but wish they weren't. They don't get on so well together. One of the girls decided that I would suit her better. The problem is that I prefer to choose my own roommate and, for all kinds of reasons, I don't choose her.

We had just about reached the point of hair pulling when, thank goodness, Ami arrived to referee and saved the day. He pointed out diplomatically that all our arrangements would come to naught in a very short time since all the students living in the Katamon district, which is considered one of the more dangerously exposed areas, will probably be transferred to our building and we will all have to double-up anyway. He undertook to find out from the University Housing Committee what it has in mind and to settle the problem for us. Now that's what I call a good neighbor.

I read in the *Post* the other day a scary item about fifty-five people being killed in New York's worst snow storm in history. It's comforting to know that Palestine isn't the only dangerous place. I hope you are all o.k.

My bones are rattling, it's so cold. Thanks for the warm underwear. Guard duty is now a little more tolerable.

Don't laugh, but I took up knitting. Learned the basic stitches in Hebrew from a friend, then had to consult the dictionary for the terminology in English in order to follow the instruction book on how to make — you guessed it — bed socks. I discovered what our grandmothers always knew, that knitting is relaxing, helps relieve the tension and makes idle hours productive.

Studying is becoming a lost cause. For two days buses have been unable to get through to Mount Scopus because of "disturbances" on the roads. It seems silly to stick out your neck unnecessarily when there is ample opportunity to risk it constructively. For the moment, most everyone, me included, has abandoned studies. As for my scholarship from the Zionist Organization of America, the money certainly hasn't been wasted. I may not be studying formally, but I sure am learning a lot of other things.

The General Post Office has been officially closed for days — no pickups or deliveries, except telegrams. The reason: there has been a succession of mail robberies on the railroads and Arab employees of the Post Office are carefully selecting and destroying all mail addressed to Jews. Whatever the fate of the mail, we certainly don't get it. But keep trying.

Love,
*Zippy*

*Jerusalem*

*January 1, 1948*

Dearest Mother, Dad and Naomi,

I can't begin to explain how different the reality of being here is from all the romantic notions I had accumulated about what life in Palestine would be like. My mental pictures of the biblical Holy Land had to do with pastoral scenes, pioneers draining swampland, cultivating the soil, reclaiming barren fields, planting trees and forests, building settlements, towns and industries and dancing joyously around a campfire after their arduous day's work. I had imagined student life was going to be a carefree time for learning Hebrew as a living language. All of this a pleasant interlude before getting to the serious business of settling down to career, family and the rest.

The contrasts between my mental pictures and the facts of life here are so jarring I cannot always relate to them. Nobody prepared me for this caldron. I was ready to rough it and not complain. But what I am being called upon to do is put my life on the line, daily and whole-heartedly. It's a little unsettling.

Speaking of mental pictures, I must digress. You know the painting we have on the wall at home showing a procession of camels, outlined sharply against the sun? Well, I haven't seen a camel since I got here. But this evening, I did see something that reminded me of them.

I came home at twilight rather shaken after a full and frightening day — I wish I could tell you what happened, but I can't. By chance, I looked up at the sky just in time to see the sun sink behind the mountains and set off a flare of red and beige that silhouetted the hills and rooftops of Jerusalem like paper cut-outs against a glowing back-ground. All that was missing were the camels. The fleeting moment passed and the red and beige faded into soft whites which seemed to frame the black rooftops and other black objects which outlined themselves on the horizon. The darkness clamped down on me with a thud, beautiful but dangerous, and I hurried into the house.

This evening, Morty R. and I collaborated on a festive supper to commemorate nothing more spectacular than being alive after a narrow escape. To celebrate, we bought a can of kosher beef, some potatoes, carrots and tomatoes, and had a great meal topped off by an honest-to-goodness can of crushed pineapple that Morty had received from home.

Now, with a cozy kerosene stove blazing and background music provided by Forces Request, mostly

American numbers, I feel the contrast sharply. The scene is so utterly incongruous. The terrifying events of today have been temporarily blocked out and, in another few hours, it will seem as if they never happened. Everything will have dissolved into a far-fetched dream I concocted — stove, radio, crushed pineapple. Hard to know what is real.

A blessed interruption: a message from the head of the Jewish Agency Youth Department, Abe Harman [subsequently Israeli ambassador to the United States; now chancellor of the Hebrew University], for whom I have been doing some part-time editorial work. He is recommending me to the editor of a weekly English news bulletin in another Agency department for additional work several days a week.

Re finances, I am holding onto my meager resources, except for what's essential for day-to-day living expenses and accumulated debts like rent. Aside from the annoyance of having to shop for food, I prefer to eat in my room or join with friends, pooling our reserves. At least that way I know what goes into my stomach and how clean it is. Not to "open my mouth to the devil," as the Hebrew saying goes, but I've been disgustingly healthy since I came, not even a sign of the occasional stomach upsets that plague the others.

Incidentally, I had to wait on line for two hours to get *neft* (kerosene) for the stove, in order to have some nice warm evenings at home for a change. I've been making it a practice to dash out in between shooting sessions, as soon as the first "all clear" sounds, to visit friends who *have* stoves going. That's one way to get popular around here.

Just realized it's New Year's Day. Happy New Year!

Love,
*Zippy*

Dearest All,

Back in the four walls of my cell tonight after a
civilized Shabbat in the lap of luxury. I feel like I used to as
a camp counselor, after a day off in the city, returning
reluctantly to roughing it with the noisy kids. Alizah and I
made the much-to-be-avoided trip downtown yesterday,
taking with us pajamas, blankets and whatnots. We'd been
invited by Morty, Milt and Ray to cook them a decent meal
and hostess a housewarming and post-New Year's Eve
party. They've rented a bachelor apartment in Rehaviah
where the author Meyer Levin lives when he is in Palestine.

I can't begin to describe what a wonderful evening we
had. Carmi joined us for supper. Alizah and I whipped up
some fantastic delicacies and managed to disguise the fact
that they had their origin in cans. I even created some
mock salads and an honest-to-goodness dessert. The boys
went crazy with delight. Since we've been here, we hadn't
enjoyed an American-style Shabbat meal together. Just the
look on everyone's faces when we lit candles made the
effort worthwhile. Afterwards, the boys washed the dishes
and cleaned up the house for the company. A whole crowd
of mutual friends joined us in the evening including Dov,
who now has a room in the city, Sally, a lot of Palestinians
and a few "Anglo-Saxons," as English-speaking people are
called here, from Rhodesia and South Africa.

The fact that the electricity was cut off for two hours
and there were a couple of other disturbances didn't
dampen our spirits at all; in fact it added to the hilarity
and incongruity of enjoying ourselves for a change.

When the company left, we sat on the rug in front of the electric stove, played records and sang until way into the night. Alizah and I got the bedroom and the boys spread out with makeshift sleeping arrangements on the couch and the floor in the living room. I hadn't slept so well since I came, a delicious sleep, without a worry in my head or the sound of gunfire in my ears.

This morning, we lounged around over a delectable breakfast and devoured the remains of the jar of Borden's powdered coffee someone had brought. After dressing and straightening up last night's mess, we held library for an hour, each of us with a book or newspaper, and then got into a political discussion (in Hebrew, no less) provoked by an article that Ray was reading on why one of the *Yishuv* leaders, Moshe Sneh, had resigned from a key post.

Dov reappeared this morning and insisted on taking Carmi and me to lunch at Jerusalem's classy hotel, the Eden, to fulfill a long-forgotten promise that we all three would eat royally as soon as he got a permanent job at the *Post*. We ate like kings, with Alizah and the boys joining us for Turkish coffee afterwards in the lounge. Then we made the rounds, visiting a few of the people who had visited us the night before and finally, bucking a raging wind, went back to the apartment for hot tea. I hated to leave. Can't afford to spoil myself this way if I want to survive in my own territory. So with heart in mouth, Alizah and I boarded the bus back to the wilds of Montefiore.

Incidentally, more than once on Friday night we found ourselves pondering the fact that here we are in the thick of things and our parents back home, most of whom know each other, would have *shepped* a little *nachas* to know that we had all been together reviving, as it were, a bit of the old home atmosphere.

Love,
*Zippy*

*January 6, 1948*

Dearest Mother and Dad,

Jerusalem is stone cold. We've had a siege of rainy weather and when it rains here it usually pours for days in succession, with the added misery of damp houses and cold driving winds that slap you in the face when you're not looking. There are still three deep-water pools outside our house from the last rainy spell. The kids in the neighborhood while away the time fishing in them and dig up odd articles — old shoes, discarded pots, etc. That or they compete with each other by tossing rocks in to see who can make the biggest splash. I keep imagining they are practicing to throw grenades.

The only thing we aren't flooded with these days is food. Milk, eggs, meat and fresh vegetables are getting hard to find. They have simply disappeared.

Yesterday, I waited in line again for hours with my tin can hoping to get *neft* for the heating stove. There's a new distribution system — a donkey cart brings a kerosene tank to the neighborhood. But neither of them ever showed up. I live in two layers of slacks with warm underwear, two tiers of sweaters over a red wool shirt, the only warm one I possess, and boots, dreaming of the day I will put on a dress again. I may be shocked to discover that I still have flesh-and-blood legs, they've been hidden under the cloth for so long.

Mount Scopus has been completely inaccessible for over a week, even for armored buses, and there are rumors of official curtailment of studies. The Americans may not be affected immediately because the University is trying to make arrangements to continue classes somehow, somewhere, probably either at the homes of the professors or at the Bet Hakerem Teachers Seminary. It's *a must.* Otherwise, the Veterans Administration might get wind of suspended studies and discontinue those helpful little GI checks. I'm told that the University representative, when asked whether or not the GIs were really studying, answered super diplomatically, "They are studying just as much as the other students are."

I've had my student visa renewed without too much difficulty. I am now officially in Palestine until October 1948. By that time I hope there'll be a Jewish State to sanction my stay. Have to stop.

Love,
*Zippy*

— *NOTE*

*I'm not so sure the British would have extended my visa had they known about my Haganah activities at that time. Among other assignments, I carried hand grenades stuffed into my blouse, while out walking supposedly guilelessly beside a Haganah man. For a Haganah man to be caught with arms by the British could have meant a* death sentence. *Women generally were not searched, so our job was to accompany the men and deliver the goods where they were needed. As I was "well-endowed," the added bulk of firearms around my waist didn't arouse suspicion, so I was much in demand for these outings.*

*One day, we were told to bring the "goods" to a place not far from the Levin-Epstein house. I had been there for Thanksgiving dinner and knew the location. What I did not know was that the area, which was uncomfortably close to the Old City, had already become*

*a front line. Hopping in and out of doorways to dodge
snipers, and crawling part of the way, we very nearly
didn't make it. I'll never forget the grateful bear-hug I
got for my delivery service.*

*Occasionally, I was assigned to substitute for an
English-speaking friend who had the tedious but
important task of eavesdropping on telephone
conversations at British HQ — via a radio hookup to
the British Police channel.*

*Jerusalem*

*January 8, 1948*

Dearest Mother, Dad and Naomi,

This is one letter I am sure will reach you because it is
going via Boston with one of the American students who is
leaving. I am told that a million eyes read our mail before
it gets to you, part of the reason for the delays. Finally, I
get an opportunity to write an *uncensored* letter and I can't
think of a damn thing to say that will make any sense to
you . . . aside from the fact that I am being rushed to finish
this even before I've started.

I don't know how to tell you not to worry about me. I
imagine that if our roles were reversed I'd be sick with
worry. There's no sense telling you that American students
are sitting on the sidelines and watching the procession of
events without participating. The truth is that most of us
are involved in some *tafkid* (assignment) or other, with
lesser or greater degrees of danger. As far as I can tell,
women have an equal status with men in the Haganah —

but they are still given low-level duties. I suspect that if the battle were only against the British, we would be more involved. The British have a reputation for being a little more gentlemanly than the Arabs when confronted with women.

The only studying I'm doing at the moment is a first aid course which meets three times a week. Trying to talk in Anatomy is a semantic torture. I know where the extremities are and am learning how to treat them in case of emergency, but oh, to spell them in Hebrew!

The other volunteer activity that keeps us all busy is *shmirah* (guard duty). My neighbor Ami, it can now be told, was our local Haganah commander and it was he who gave me firsthand instruction on the arms we would be using. How to aim, fire and clean them — blindfolded. It seems I have a special knack with His Majesty's hardware. Now I'm passing on what I learned to the others. After a while, Ami was taken for more important things and replaced by Yehudah. So when I mention their names you will know who is who. With all this personal tutelage on the fine art of defending myself, I'd like to see a Manhattan masher start up with me now.

I was just interrupted by Yehudah, who popped in to invite me to a movie — as soon as he gets a night off, that is, which can be anywhere from tomorrow to a month. It's called planning ahead. This guy is something. He leaves me notes with sweet little nothings written on them in the most ungrammatical English, learned in His Majesty's Service, and expects me to correct them. On duty, he pops out from behind dark trees to test my quick reaction. Somehow, Naomi, he reminds me, of your *shaliach* friend D., a kind of "he-man"–little boy combination, only Y. is more polished and has the credentials of a third-generation Sabra.

Nary a night goes by when he doesn't pop in a dimpled face to coo good night at me and see if I'm all right. Once the head is past the partly open door and has been smilingly received, the rest of him wiggles in and sits itself down at the table. He reaches for the Bible — he is trying to improve my Hebrew — and opens to the chapter following the one we read the previous night. He reads, then explains. I ask questions, he answers. He finishes reading. Then I read from an old *New Yorker* magazine or an anthology of modern American poetry in an effort to improve his English. He listens, asks questions, I explain. I finish reading. He says good night. That, in short, is our romance — plus an occasional movie or a walk through the hills when we are on duty together.

He has nicknamed his tommy gun after me and loads it "with little twinklings from the laughter in my eyes." Get that, willya? I am now near famous in the neighborhood in a very unflattering way because of him. Word is passed around that Zippy (or "Tzipke," as the gun is called), will be getting a workout at such and such a time and place. Actually, it is an official code message for a clandestine Haganah action. The next day, I am asked in fun: "How was it?" All I can do is blush demurely because I participated in the activity in name only, though I'm told my namesake wasn't found wanting.

I guess all this sounds very ominous, but it is part of life here and a fascinating experience. Carmi and I were just commenting the other day on the fact that it's a helluva way to spend a year of study and certainly not what the ZOA had in mind when they granted us the scholarships. We decided, laughingly, that if we ever get back to studying they'll have to increase the tuition allowance. We won't settle for anything less than $1,500 because the cost of living — not to speak of staying alive — has increased considerably.

Like most of my letters, this is being written to the accompaniment of an unrelenting background of gunpowder explosion, like a sound track to a film. I am intently banging away at the typewriter, dunking cookies in tea and mashing out cigarettes, and every so often I stop short, wondering why it is suddenly quiet, why the shooting has stopped. What has happened? Mostly you don't bat an eyelash while the volley is going on, your ear muscles condition themselves to pick up the refrain and measure the distance. It's when it stops suddenly that you get concerned.

Have to finish. The courier is leaving. I almost wish I were going with this letter, but I'd hate to miss what's happening here.

Love,
*Zippy*

*Jerusalem*

*January 15, 1948*

Dearest Wonderful Family,

Finally, the first letter from you in over a month. It was so good to hear from you. And it took only five days to arrive. Probably, when the Post Office reopened the other day, after suspending service for so long, they tackled all the new mail and are holding the backlog for distribution later — in another millennium or never. At least, I know you are all well and still thinking of me. As for notices about the packages you sent, they are probably lost forever in the batch of mail stolen around Christmas time. Knowing the name of the boat bearing my precious cargo doesn't help because boats land in Haifa and Tel Aviv and I am in Jerusalem, a planet and light years away. In the future, please send things via Parcel Post; it's more direct and just might arrive. Oh, for a can of tuna fish and a jar of coffee.

I just glanced at my fingers pattering over the keys. I've got a first-class case of dishpan hands. The laundryman took a powder about a month ago and disappeared, along with my khaki skirt, three sheets, pillow cases and towels. He is no longer at his old address and is probably scared to venture out to the backwoods where we live. So, out of sheer necessity I had to wash everything by hand, sheets included. Can you believe it? I'm going to track him down as soon as I get a chance and claim my stuff. He's a nice little man with a long grey beard and I am sure he didn't intentionally walk off with my wash. Must be ill or something.

My local hero, Yehudah, had a few hours off tonight and took me to the movies in style. As he had ordered the tickets in advance, I didn't want to spoil his fun by telling him that I had already seen the picture — *The Farmer's Daughter*. It wasn't so bad having to see it again. Better than sitting at home.

Out of desperation I gave myself a haircut this afternoon — a little too short, but suits me. Also, the knitting is doing fine. One bed sock is finished, the second is coming up slowly.

That's it for now. It's late.

Love,<br>
*Zippy*

Naomi Dear,

Many of the American students, unable to study and unwilling to get "involved," are returning to the U.S., making it doubly hard on those of us who remain. The Jews in Palestine recognize only one kind of Zionist, one who comes here ready to do what must be done to make the Jewish Homeland a permanent fact. Now that we have a chance to stand side by side with them in a real struggle to do just that, they cannot understand the readiness to leave. I don't understand it myself. We have waited two thousand years for this chance. I certainly want to be around while it's happening. Unless people come to populate this country, and stay, a Jewish State will be only a paper plan.

The situation is very tense and probably will continue to be until the British leave — a hundred thousand British troops in the country and they are unable to maintain order. Instead, they are abetting and inciting the Arabs at every turn. The British Army, the British Police and the Arab Legion led by British officers: they are the enemy, not the Arab peoples. I am sure we will muddle through somehow, but a little help from America wouldn't hurt, and not just money.

It becomes clearer and clearer to me how misguided you and other American Zionists are. You waste so much effort on mass actions, mass appeals, mass protests. Why not leave the masses alone for a while and concentrate on influencing individuals — young people who might respond to a call to serve their nation. Americans have so much to give that is so desperately needed here. But be careful whom you send. They had better be people willing to accept the challenge and able to adjust to the difficult life they will find here — people with stickability and a sense of purpose.

Being in Palestine at this time is a little like a wild west adventure; it is pioneering in every sense of the word. To be part of it, you don't necessarily have to be in a kibbutz. Any covered wagon will do. The Indians are all around — only here they are dressed like Arabs and British policemen.

Love,
*Zippy*

*Later the same day . . .*

I had just typed the words *later the same day* when BANG went the windows, the doors shook and the typewriter almost fell off the table. I ran outside to see what had happened, only to discover that building workers were blasting down the street to prepare a building site. In America, at least they yell "timber" first. So, for people considering coming to this country, add a strong nervous system to the criteria mentioned above.

*Jerusalem*

*January 19, 1948*

Dearest Everybody,

Jerusalem's face was sad today. It isn't easy to accept the fact of death, and even harder when you know personally many of those who died. But *thirty-five boys* is heartbreaking, all young wonderful people. The thirty-five Haganah fighters, mostly university students, were sent to relieve the besieged Gush Etzion kibbutzim and were massacred by the Arabs while the British stood by without intervening.

I can imagine that the death of Moshe Pearlstein from New York, my friend Marsha's brother, must have created a wave of shock; the first American to be killed here. I went racing around madly last night trying to catch Donovan of NBC who covers the Palestine scene for the news round-up. Someone tipped me off that he expected to give details and names and, as far as I knew, the family had not yet been notified. It would have been awful for them to hear it that way. Finally, an Associated Press friend saw to it that the report was made with as much discretion as possible. The American group here is grieved. Moshe was a great guy.

Oded was also among the dead. You remember I mentioned him in earlier letters. He was one of the first Sabras to befriend me. In fact, when I first arrived he took me on an excursion to that very area and hiked me over those hills to visit the kibbutzim in Gush Etzion so I would learn to love the land as he did. Just before he left for this assignment, he came to say hello and we talked at length, as always arguing in earnest about . . . Oh, hell, what's the difference now!

Your daughter,
*Zippy*

---

*Jerusalem*

*January 24, 1948*

Dearest Mother and Dad,

Am planning to call you in two weeks on your anniversary. As I understand the routine, I have to contact the overseas operator at least three days beforehand so that she can notify you in New York when to expect the call. It costs about three-and-a-half Palestine Pounds (over fifteen dollars) for three minutes.

Let's not waste time saying "Hello. Hello. Hello. How are you?" Obviously I'm fine if I'm calling. And please don't ask me questions about the political situation, etc., because the wires are tapped. The main thing is to hear each other's voices. I hope the reception will be good. Incidentally, I am sending special regards and maybe a few trinkets with two fellows who are coming to New York as *shlichim*. They are both students at the new improvised Diplomats School in Bet Hakerem where high-ranking civil servants will be trained as ambassadors and such in the foreign service of the upcoming State. How I met them is a story in itself.

One day, my Haganah commander assigned me to do a couple of hours of lookout duty, the straining job of spyglassing the activities of the neighboring Arab villages — counting and recording incoming and outgoing people and vehicles. I was told to go to a room in the Diplomats School because the view from the window there was excellent. When I reported for duty at 6:00 A.M. I found the two occupants of the room fast asleep, so I moved about as quietly as I could, found a good position, took up my spyglass and got to work — and never saw the astonishment on their faces when they woke up an hour later and found Mata Hari sitting at the window.

Over a cup of tea after duty, I found out that they were leaving shortly for the States to take up assignments as *shlichim* to the Zionist youth movements: one of them was going to my friends in Plugat Aliyah. Then came the best part of the story. The letter they showed me inviting them to New York and instructing them on their assignments was signed by none other than MY OWN SISTER, Naomi, representing the Chalutziut Commission. How is that for coincidence?

Yehudah dropped in for tea and sympathy and to bring me up to date on what's going on in Jerusalem and the rest of the country. He is my talking newspaper and always has inside information which turns out to be remarkably reliable. He's fallen asleep in the chair, exhausted after two consecutive nights accompanying convoys in and out of the city. The British are doing nothing to stop the Arabs from terrorizing the road and ambushing our supplies. So, *we* have to keep the communication lines open between Jerusalem and the rest of the country. If we don't, the State will be lost before it is born.

I haven't the heart to continue typing lest I wake him, so this will have to suffice for the time being.

Love,
*Zippy*

*Jerusalem*

*January 26, 1948*

Dear Naomi,

Abba Hillel Silver, your chief Zionist spokesman, was just here on a visit. In an interview with an American correspondent he expressed considerable annoyance at the fact that he, AN AMERICAN CITIZEN, had to be subjected to the uncomfortable trip in an armored bus from Lydda to Jerusalem. He wanted to know why the British couldn't secure the road for him. We would all like to know that. Once the shooting starts it hardly matters how important you are or what your citizenship is. Bullets are notoriously indiscriminating.

The day he left he had a powwow with us, about forty American ex-servicemen and Zionist youth leaders. We were ushered into one of the inner-sanctum conference rooms at the Jewish Agency building. The best thing about the two hours was the tea they served and the thought that Ben-Gurion had warmed up the chair for me. Silver, with a noticeable degree of vagueness, answered the questions we put to him about the problems of American Zionist *chalutziut* (pioneering activities) and American participation in defense measures here. Not once did he stroke his monumental mop of hair, as he usually does. He just kept shifting the ponderous weight of his "corporation" from side to side with every uncomfortable question we put to him.

He explained that he was leaving in a hurry because he had to return to the U.S. to see what could be done about the State Department's latest tendency to press for a special UN Assembly meeting to re-discuss the Partition Plan. You know what that'll mean, of course; more stalling and indecision which may upset the apple cart.

Sorry I can't get to the kibbutz to visit our friends. It's the policy these days to keep to your own area and not travel around unless it's urgent, on duty, or unavoidable.

Love,
*Zippy*

*Jerusalem*

*January 30, 1948*

Dear Everybody,

I've been walking around for days with two notices in my purse about packages which arrived but I haven't gotten up enough courage and fast walking power to make it to the General Post Office and back in one breath. To release the parcels, I have to show up in person and, as I keep telling you, the P.O. is located in a predominantly Arab sector which makes it a dangerous place to go. But today, I mentioned the problem to a friend I met in the street and he insisted on accompanying me. Boy, was I glad to have him along, not only to hold my hand because I was a bit scared, but also to help carry the loot.

Wow! Cigarettes, tuna fish, fruit, powdered chicken soup, powdered coffee, powdered milk, powdered eggs, powdered everything — all that was missing was gun powder. The kids went wild, full of praise for my wonderful family. We pulled out one item at a time, lolled over it, discussed the last time we had tasted it and began to argue about whom we should invite to share a meal; so many people have been nice to us. Everything arrived in super condition, with the exception of a jar of coffee which broke and formed a muddy paste on one side of the carton.

Rachie, Alizah and I have pooled the contents of our food parcels and set up a cooperative kitchen in my room, where the storehouse is. Alizah, who was a dietician in the American Army, is very inventive at making something from nothing and has gone on a cooking spree. She cooks and we take turns washing up and scrounging for food, which is a very time-consuming, frustrating business considering the little that you find to bring back. Food is not only in short supply, it is very expensive — especially if you're not working. Meat is no longer obtainable.

The word "chicken" has been temporarily removed from my vocabulary because I haven't seen a dead one yet. The live ones give eggs, which are also in short supply. It isn't that there are fewer egg-laying chickens, it's just that they don't like laying eggs when they are disturbed by gunfire. In addition, transportation between the rural areas and Jerusalem is completely gummed up.

Anyhow, the pooling arrangement is great, though I wonder how long ingenuity can substitute for nutrition. We come home in the evening and find a decent meal, concocted of odd vegetables and occasional fish, or a pot full of warm, nourishing soup. It saves us all extra bus fares, and possibly our lives, because the bus to town passes through Romema which is partially Arab territory. The only problem with the arrangement is mathematical: Alizah's Army recipes are for A HUNDRED portions or more.

Love,
*Zippy*

## Part Four

# The Worst is Yet to Come

*February 3, 1948*

Dearest All,

I was stunned when I heard about last night's big bang — a direct and dastardly hit on the *Palestine Post* building, which is smack in the center of Jerusalem on Hasolel Street, just off Zion Square. Apparently, it was done by a booby-trapped British police van driven by two Englishmen.

I hurried over first thing this morning to visit Morty and Dov who work there and found them at home on the porch wrapped in blankets, devouring hot tea and cognac. Dov was grazed on the head by some flying glass, but aside from that they are fine. Lucky guys. I could imagine what they went through, after listening to their stories about the flames and chaos in the press room and helping to drag the wounded out of the smoke-clogged building.

They had been up all night because, despite the fact that the building was a shambles, the Editor and staff were determined to get the paper out in some form. They found another press and worked through the night — partly from memory and partly from scraps of carbon copies pulled out of the debris. By 6:00 this morning the *Palestine Post* — a valiant, bedraggled one-page issue — was on the streets, as usual. A fantastic feat and wonderful for everyone's morale.

I forgot to tell you that I have had to reshuffle my living quarters. With most of the American group gone, our building was vacated to make room for a school for handicapped children who had to be evacuated from a danger zone. I am now, literally, back to where I started, with all the other Americans in Pension Pax, where there is blessed hot water and a telephone. I can't complain, as I've been given a very nice room, vacated by a couple who are playing it safer by moving to town.

I suppose you have heard or read in the papers that the American Consulate has "warned" us that Americans joining the Haganah will have their passports recalled, to be returned only for purposes of travel to the States: a one-way trip. After the death of Moshe Pearlstein at Gush Etzion, they discovered that GIs were indeed participating in Haganah activities. A name on a list of dead people is sure proof. But they'll have a devil of a time proving the participation of anyone who is alive and kicking. So none of us are terribly worried. As for the American government providing protection for its citizens, that's a joke. The Consulate is smack in the heart of Arab territory and completely inaccessible for Jews, so whom are they protecting and how?

The days are moving very slowly. No classes have been organized yet and the mood to study is waning with every day that passes.

Love,
*Zippy*

—— NOTE ——————————————————————

*The tension that gripped the city during that period was frightening. For the American students, it was a grim signal either to pack up and go home or join the forces being organized to defend Jerusalem. Those of us who remained felt immense pride and privilege to be part of that heroic struggle.*

Dearest Mother, Dad and Naomi,

This morning is truly biblical weather, the story of Noah's Ark and the flood reenacted. The rain has been falling all night slapping at the earth and stones. This morning it is still pounding at the doors and windows but with gentle stinging strokes.

Yesterday was also a biblical day — a grand Exodus of American students back to "the land of the free and the home of the brave." Mothers and fathers have suddenly developed critical heart attacks and are sending cables demanding the immediate return of their offspring. Those students who don't have any ideological ties are going. The rest of us are here to stay, come what may. It seems to me that *we* have to make the decision — to stay or to leave — without parental pressure. I am very proud of you. Not a frantic word yet.

I know you are concerned and that distance and sensational news reports about the explosive security situation intensify your concern. I can only assure you that we are taking every precaution. Also, the Haganah is doing a terrific job of protecting us. If this is what it is capable of as an illegal defense force, imagine its potential as a national army.

I am aware that I constantly write in generalities. I am unable to be more specific: in some cases for reasons of security, but mostly because I find it extremely difficult to talk about a situation which is impossible for you to relate to. Not being here, you cannot really understand what we are experiencing and the picture you form in your mind's eye will inevitably be blurred and distorted. So I confine myself to small talk. I, on the other hand, am too close to what's happening, too out of perspective to be able to properly evaluate events. Yet they are indelibly etched into my consciousness.

Coming to the reality of Palestine with a Zionist background, you discover a sense of fulfillment you didn't think your life's days would contain. Sometimes, it doesn't hit you until your Americanisms have worn off a bit. Sometimes, personal problems in adjusting to the language, the people or the lack of physical comforts, cloud the picture. But, eventually, you can't help noticing that there is something special about this place and the people who live here. Even if you can't put your finger on it, you sense it. I wouldn't exchange this period in my life and this feeling of LIVING for all the comforts and security of America.

Love,
*Zippy*

*Jerusalem*

*February 10, 1948*

Dearest All,

I still can't get over the excitement of hearing your familiar voices bridging thousands of miles and reaching me clearly. I don't suppose it was important that we said nothing in particular, but the awareness that you were close, closer than letters or pictures can bring you, was very gratifying. I'm sure you felt the same.

Yesterday was one of the worst of the stormy days we've had recently. And I do mean the weather. The wind was on a wild rampage. The electricity lines were down and I was sure that the telephone service would be disconnected or full of static. So I had almost abandoned the idea of receiving the call as scheduled.

Rachie, Alizah and I had just finished supper and were snuggling up to the stove trying to warm ourselves. The witching hour — 6:00 P.M. — arrived and passed. With a disappointed sigh, I reached for more dessert. Not twenty minutes later, I heard Carmi shouting "ZIPPY!" I raced down the stairs as if on a roller coaster.

"Your call to New York is ready. Go ahead." And there you were.

"Hello, hello, hello!" I could also hear the censor clicking his teeth together in anticipation of some unwitting giveaway.

I came back upstairs with glistening eyes, smiling radiantly, and all the kids crowded around me to share the reaction and get the latest news. We are really like one big family, all involved with each other's lives. Sometimes it can be a pain in the neck, like lately.

I met a guy on duty one night who is a cross between Tyrone Power and Spencer Tracy — a pipe man with a very handsome face and soulful eyes, a journalist named Moshe. The girls are green with envy. One word led to another and I was drafted to help him edit an article he was preparing for an American magazine, though he really doesn't need my help; a second-generation Sabra, but his English is impeccable. He lives only a few houses away and came over the other night to invite me out.

I had just returned from my first aid course, was dead tired and probably looked it, and explained that I couldn't go out this week because I had an article to translate and summarize, a special request job that I had promised to do. It was a very complicated piece on the economic aspects of labor distribution of the *Yishuv*. I hadn't gotten much further than the title. But this guy read it through, helped me translate the entire thing and explained all the nuances I hadn't even understood.

In short, my social life is getting out of hand. All my good friends know each other. Too many is almost as bad as none at all.

Incidentally, there was an announcement on the radio the other day that in preparation for the British pullout from Palestine, government postal services will be discontinued, starting with *Parcel Post, as of March 15th*, except for whatever is already in transit. Parcels which aren't collected immediately will be confiscated or returned to point of origin. For the present, airmail will continue — as chaotically as ever — although for how much longer nobody knows . . .

Love,
*Zippy*

## Jerusalem

### February 14, 1948

Dearest All,

Since I arrived here, and especially since the twenty-ninth of November, Jews have had no access to most of the holy, historic or important places in Jerusalem: the Wailing Wall, the Old City, the King David Hotel area, etc. I've never even seen them, living where we do on the outskirts of town, confined to just a few of the Jewish neighborhoods. I haven't had a chance to really get the feel of the city.

But last night, Friday, I was invited by Moshe to join his family for dinner. Sitting around the table, they held me spellbound telling stories and legends about the Jerusalem of fifty years ago. Today, some of those stories came to life, and for the first time I saw Jerusalem in an entirely new light.

Starting out at about 2:00 in the afternoon, and avoiding snipers, Moshe and I hiked over the hills toward town. We were able to go straight through Romema because the Haganah has now cleared it of Arabs. Until about two weeks ago it was a hotbed of hostility, with our buses constantly under fire. I understand the Arabs left en masse, under the protection of the Haganah, who were protecting them from the extreme activists, the Irgun and the Stern Gang, and that before leaving many of them sold their belongings to their Jewish neighbors. Moshe gave me a cook's tour of the place. He knew every nook and cranny of it, having lived there as a child.

Skirting the British barracks, we took a back road and landed up in Tel Arza, a charming little community. In the town square, which was more like a huge lot, there was a lively group of children, clapping their hands, singing and dancing. Back in America I was always told that in Palestine everyone danced in the streets, but until now, I hadn't seen any spontaneous merriment.

It was a brisk, bright day, and we continued our walk, at a comfortable pace, through intricate back roads into Mea Shearim, a fascinating spot. The Jerusalem of the picture books — *streimels* (fur-trimmed hats worn by Hasidim on Sabbath and holidays) and faces framed by *peyot* (earlocks). The narrow, cobblestoned streets seemed to mushroom out of a labyrinth of courtyards. On every block there were *shtiebels* (small study and prayer centers) and every Jew looked like a venerable Moses. I thought I was back in Boro Park.

Moshe seemed to know everyone. I met the undertaker and the Rabbi, also his grandmother who is a hundred years old. He pointed out the moneylender, the cobbler and the local *meshugener* (looney), with ragged clothes and toothless face, followed by a train of scrawny children jeering at him. I felt as if the ghettos of Poland and Russia were closing in on me . . . the Eastern European clothing, the crowded courtyards and cluttered hovels, the intense eyes, the forest of beards, gesticulating hands and chanting voices greeting each other with *"Gut Shabbes"* — all this made me feel as if I were in a different world.

Suddenly, from not too far off, there were shots which brought me back to this world quickly enough. In a flash, the expressions on the faces of those around me changed, eyes were cautious with concern, lips chanted prayers, possibly begging God to get into the act.

Making our way through the narrow streets, we came to the high wall that encircles the Ethiopian community. Moshe explained to the caretaker that we wanted only a peek at the Church. As we stood there waiting for him to get the key, several black-faced, black-clad people passed us, knelt and kissed the stone stairs reverently. We entered the building silently, looking in awe at the glorious murals of multi-colored figures that stared down at us from every beam and wall. The ceiling was dome-shaped, haze-colored, like the planetarium: on it were painted angels and astrological symbols in brilliant colors. This was the anteroom; the praying is done in a closet-like chamber filled with an altar and precious objects. We passed the High Priest's throne and an impressive carpet, and then out into the light of day.

It seemed to me that we were walking in circles, but we managed to get to the center of town in time to see ambulances on Hasolel Street — probably, with the victims of the very shots we had heard not an hour ago. Passing

Zion Square, we headed toward the Moslem Cemetery (the worst place to be) for a better view of the YMCA and the King David Hotel, but the shooting sounded too close for comfort so we returned to the downtown area.

I had forgotten my identity card and, when I saw Home Guard units stationed in front of the Eden Hotel, I thought surely I would be detained. They were there because the other day somebody had threatened to blow up the hotel. But Moshe knew the guards on duty and vouched for me, so we got by. It was already about 4:30 P.M. and, needing a hot drink, we went looking for a "safe" cafe. There are very few cafes open on Shabbat since our Jewish SS men ( *"Shomrei Shabbat,"* Guardians of the Sabbath) have taken to throwing stones at such places to ensure that they show proper respect by closing on the Sabbath. It isn't clear to me which violation is bigger: stone throwing or staying open.

The minute I stepped into Cafe Europa, I felt as if I were in a speakeasy — a loud percussion band playing a tango and reddish-blue lights on a sleazy dance floor. For some reason, there were bright green-and-white-checked tablecloths. We landed up in a booth on the balcony, sitting on a red plush-lined semi-circular seat that gave me the feeling of being in a harem. After drinking some delicious Turkish coffee, we made for the dance floor. Moshe had warned me that he wasn't a good dancer, but, oh, how he lied. It was heavenly to be dancing tangos, rumbas, fox trots — the works. But, it was so weird. I couldn't believe that this, too, was Jerusalem.

Off in a corner, the Haganah boys were nursing their guns as if we already had a Jewish State and no precautions were necessary. When they got up to dance, they just left the guns on the table. The waiter passed by and discreetly covered them up.

And, of all the incongruities, just about the time when *Havdalah* (end-of-Sabbath prayer) would have been said, the band played the appropriate song to mark the end of Shabbat, *"Shavua Tov,"* and everybody joined in. I couldn't take it all in; too many contrasts for one day.

*Zippy*

---

*Jerusalem*

*February 18, 1948*

Naomi Dear,

The guy who is being sent to America to serve as a *shaliach* to Plugat Aliyah was here this morning to say good-bye. You remember I wrote you how I met him in his room at the Diplomats School while on lookout duty.

I think he'll do very well. He is rather quiet, thoughtful, objective, clear-thinking, earnest, personable and, most important, honest with himself. He has heard many confusing and conflicting stories about America from our people here. He listened attentively, digested the information and is reserving judgment until he gets on the scene — very diplomatic. He's not the fiery enthusiastic type, but I think he will accomplish a great deal and talk a great deal less about it than some people we know.

Before going, he'll spend a few days in Kibbutz Ginegar with our people there, so that by the time he leaves he will be pretty well-briefed. Members of Plugat Aliyah in Jerusalem met in my room last night for a session with him. About fifteen people were present. Abe Harman, the Head of the Jewish Agency Youth Department, spoke. It was an excellent meeting. I'll send minutes and other details along as soon as I can.

Events are developing here so rapidly and with such intensity that I am unable to answer your questions about the pros and cons of *chalutziut*. That kind of dialogue is utterly removed from our day-to-day activities. It takes every ounce of pioneering stamina to live in Palestine at all in these times.

I can tell you that, in my opinion, the only kind of *chalutziut* is *the act of arrival*. Anything short of that is Zionist propaganda talking to itself. Adjustment to this country doesn't really depend on exposure to youth movement training farms or, for that matter, a Zionist background or knowledge of Hebrew. It doesn't hurt to have all that behind you, but mainly it depends on individual personality, durability and determination not to be put off by the difficulties. Not everybody can take this rugged life. You have to be able to look squarely at all the shortcomings of this country — backwardness, ignorance, inefficiency, etc. — and discern its one outstanding attribute: *it is the Jewish National Homeland*, the only one we have.

It's also a unique kind of society, where *people* count, not the things they own or represent, where money is unable to buy what makes life meaningful. What's the price for peace of mind, personal safety?

*Zippy*


*Jerusalem*

*February 22, 1948*

Dearest Family,

I was awakened by a shattering explosion at about 6:45 this morning, turned over and dreamed the noise into a restless dream. Then the awareness that it was real hit me full blast. I hopped out of bed, pounded down the stairs to the telephone and got through to a friend who was in such a state of shock she could hardly tell me what had happened.

It seems the damn British, or Arabs dressed in British uniform, drove up in three lorries filled with explosives which they set off in the center of Jerusalem's downtown section, Ben-Yehudah Street, the busiest and liveliest street in town. This, at an hour when people go to work or are still at home, in an area crammed with crowded apartments, office buildings and shops.

Everyone coming from town assures me that it's better to stay home because you can't get within a yell of the place and will only interfere with efforts to clear the debris and find survivors. No way of knowing yet the number of casualties. [It was reported later that there were over 50 dead and some 170 wounded.]

*Later the same day . . .*

I went to town this afternoon. What devastation, what destruction! Even several blocks away, on King George V Street, the roofs are a shambles, entire storefronts are blasted away, the streets are a mass of glass and debris. Standing in the middle of one pile was my groceryman, collecting "Mazal tovs" for being alive. Not a window, not a sign, not an undamaged building in the entire area. It is frustrating to think that these are the very same windows and the very same buildings that were repaired barely two weeks ago after the blasting of the press room of the *Palestine Post*, not three blocks away.

Every main street, with the exception of two blocks on Jaffa Road, is cut off to the public by the linked arms of *Mishmar Ha'am*, volunteer Jewish Home Guard units, who form a cordon to protect the stricken area. This was one day when British soldiers and policemen scarcely showed themselves in the streets of the city. They would have been attacked by mobs of furious people. I might have been among them myself.

What kind of a crazy war is this? Whom are we fighting? Who is neutral? Who is on our side? How much provocation are we supposed to take before retaliating? We know the price of paying back, but how long can it restrain us? We are like sitting ducks in a shooting gallery. And there is so little we can do about it; not even permitted to protect ourselves. The people who live here have super-human guts and patience to absorb blow after blow — from the Arabs, from the British, from all sides. I know that on *shmirah* (guard duty) tonight I'll be gripping the sten gun just a little bit more firmly, for it is events like this that ignite the kind of burning anger which can transform even a peace-loving person into a fighter, a soldier.

Jerusalem is very small, so that anything that hits, hits everything indiscriminately — residential areas, commercial areas, hospitals and schools. If you glance at a map of the city, you'll notice that Jerusalem proper, the new city, is only ten or twelve blocks in circumference.

It is bounded to the south by "Bevingrad," nicknamed after Britain's Foreign Secretary Ernest Bevin. This is a huge compound, encircled by barbed wire, containing not only all the important British administration offices, police headquarters, the courts, the prison, hospital, banks, the broadcasting station, but also the Jewish commercial area, the Arab sector and the General Post Office, which services everybody.

To the west is Rehaviah, a lovely residential quarter where the Jewish Agency building is located. To the north is Mahaneh Yehudah, the less affluent part of the city where there is a bustling marketplace that overflows into the Orthodox communities. Continuing farther in this direction is Romema, a mixed Jewish/Arab sector — previously predominantly Arab — and then round the bend is Kiryat Moshe (New Montefiore), where we live, and Bet Hakerem, where other student quarters are. Spread out behind Kiryat Moshe there are two Arab villages, Deir Yassin and Lifta, and the Jewish suburb Givat Shaul.

Come to think of it, we are actually closer to the center of the city than our house on 83rd Street is to Times Square. Only passing through Romema on the bus — at least, until recently — was a nerve-racking hit-or-miss affair, spiked by snipers. It bore no resemblance to a Fifth Avenue bus ride.

Strategically, we are more or less safe. The only thing we have to fear is an out-and-out full-scale attack by the Arabs, which isn't likely because they know how strong and united we are and we know their every movement.

I am stressing the geography so that when you read all sorts of disturbing and frightening news about Jerusalem, you should realize that the city is made up of a hundred or more suburb-like communities and, at this stage, only some of them are under constant or sporadic fire. It doesn't necessarily mean that we students are in the thick of things *all* the time.

Jerusalem is a difficult city to live in and to protect. The Jewish sections are not exclusively Jewish, nor the Arab sections entirely Arab, nor the British zones strictly British. The hardest part is getting about from one section to another and trying to protect the Jewish inhabitants who happen to live in a mixed section. And, a major overall problem is to protect ourselves from the British who are free to come and go as they please.

Jewish Home Guard roadblocks can stop and examine a car or a truck that looks suspicious but they cannot intercept a British Army or Police vehicle, even if there were proof positive that it contained explosives destined for detonation in a Jewish area. And that's the background on how the *Palestine Post* building and Ben-Yehudah Street got bombed.

*Zippy*

*Jerusalem*

*February 24, 1948*

Dearest All,

It seems I finished my first aid course just in time to be useful. I decided not to wait for official assignments, everything is done in such a partisan manner anyhow. So yesterday, waving my Magen David Adom (Jewish "Red Cross") arm band, I somehow pushed through the cordons to the stricken area on Ben-Yehudah Street. No question about it, every extra hand was needed.

Excavations were still going on to unearth survivors trapped under the rubble and debris. Dazed people, some of them with wounds, were wandering around looking for relatives. Nobody was attending to them — in all the pandemonium it was hard to find the first aid stations. I simply set up one of my own.

In a prominent place, on a sheltered doorway, I drew a big Magen David Adom with my lipstick; before I knew it I was in business. The workers from Solel Boneh, digging in the ruins, came in to have cuts and abrasions treated. I collected a group of children, some of them in an awful state, who were wandering about waiting to hear word of their parents. There was plenty to do.

Are there words to describe senseless human tragedy? Will I, can I, ever forget this day? I am becoming like the Jews who live here: every shock and sorrow nurtures them to grim restraint and fierce dedication.

Love,
*Zippy*

*Jerusalem*

*February 28, 1948*

Naomi Dear,

Even though it's only 8:00 P.M., I've just crawled into bed — my lumpy straw mattress — which, tonight, feels great because I haven't slept at all for two nights. I've been busy with "community activities" — that's what defending Jerusalem is called these days.

Am writing by flashlight so as not to disturb a woman who is sleeping in the extra bed in my room — a Rumanian lady of about fifty, who doesn't speak a word of Hebrew, English, French or anything else I can converse in. She talks at me in German and I respond in sign language, body talk and smiles.

When I was doing first aid at the Ben-Yehudah Street bombing site, I found her wandering around, slightly wounded and very disoriented. While I bandaged her wound, she told me she had lost her entire family in the Holocaust. Now, the house on Ben-Yehudah Street where she lived and worked has been reduced to rubble and she has no place to stay. She has kind of attached herself to me and I'm not yet able to direct her to official agencies for help. I don't know where they are myself.

So, I tried to make some temporary arrangement with our landlady to let her sleep here for a couple of nights. But, the landlady reneged at the last moment, for whatever reason, after having agreed to the arrangement. I couldn't turn the woman out: it was bitter cold, so I smuggled her into my room, for tonight at least.

She was so grateful. For what — a straw mattress, a clean bandage, a bite to eat and a cup of hot tea. To her, at that moment, a whole world.

Love,
*Zippy*

*Jerusalem*

*March 1, 1948*

Dearest Everybody,

I finally finished my first aid course, formally. I have to confess — but don't tell anybody — that I hadn't really completed the course when I took to the field. Last night I had my final exam and passed with flying colors. I consider it a real victory. Basically, it was very technical material in a brand-new language; some of the terms have only just been coined. Most of the time, I had to search my dictionary frantically to find the parts of the body being discussed and their functions, praying that my patient wouldn't expire before I learned the name of his ailment. But, on the exam, I did magnificently and am very proud of myself. The doctor in charge of the course said he couldn't find a single mistake, not even in spelling.

I didn't tell him that I had already been practicing first aid, even before I had finished the two-month course. In this fantastic country you find yourself doing lots of things you never in your wildest dreams thought you could or would be doing. I am now a full-fledged *choveshet*, literally a dresser of wounds, which is a first aid "nurse." So, next time you break a leg, send for me.

This country is super-ultra-vulnerable. In America, I always thought world politics was something exclusively for the experts in the ivory towers to study under a magnifying glass. It was their job to analyze events and pronounce unsettling developments in some remote part of the globe as a potential threat; the more remote, the bigger the threat. After reading the news, I would hurriedly finish my coffee, put down the paper and go about my business. Let them deal with the threat.

Here, perhaps because the country is so small, the goings-on in every other country, especially the neighboring ones, become vitally important, not just as a remote threat but as a frightening reality. You find yourself watching world events with increasing awareness and mounting anxiety, suddenly conscious of the fact that your perspective has very much changed.

Love,
*Zippy*


*Jerusalem*

*March 3, 1948*

Dear Everybody,

Studying at the University is now totally impossible. Instead, I have joined a course which the Jewish Agency has arranged for Anglo-Saxon girls — from England, South

Africa, America and Canada — who have had some social work background and have come to work with *plitim* (refugees) and *olim chadashim,* (new immigrants). It is sponsored by the Vaad Leumi (the Jewish governing body) and is being held at the Henrietta Szold Jewish Welfare Institute.

Today's lesson was extraordinarily interesting. The lecturer was the Mandatory government's Chief Probation Officer, who spoke to us on the problems and treatment of Arab and Jewish juvenile delinquency. After the lecture, the first social worker in the country, Zipporah Bloch (one of Henrietta Szold's "girls"), took us on a tour of settlement houses, particularly those in the "safe" sections of Jerusalem.

We went first to Nachalat Zion to the Hadassah Infant Welfare Station. You could spot it three blocks away: all the windows of Hadassah buildings are painted blue. It wasn't anything like the Jacob Schiff Center. It was just a dilapidated apartment in a decrepit house but renovated, spotlessly clean and reconverted to serve as a demonstration and health center for pregnant women, mothers and infants. The woman in charge was a legend in herself. She ran the first such station in the Old City of Jerusalem when dirt was fatal and ignorance prevailed. She speaks Turkish and all the other oriental languages of the patients she treats. The little apartment was scrubbed up and gaily decorated with charming pictures and instructive charts. From there, we walked through the street where every two steps Miss Bloch was stopped by a familiar face and invited in to see "how clean we keep our home."

Just as we were visiting one of the clinics, we overheard a Group Leader telling the women in a Mothers Group how to handle children during bombings and other disturbances — how to keep them from feeling insecure and frightened,

111

how to amuse them, sing with them and take their minds off what is happening.

In another community we visited, the people live very primitively, ten or fifteen members of a family in ONE room, a dirty, damp, cluttered room, with an outhouse and a closet of a kitchen, both outside. Scores of skinny, scantily-clad youngsters, with diseased faces and dripping noses, were running about in the cobbled alleys and paths that connect the "streets." And these ARE NOT the poorest families. This is not a slum area.

There is no law or social pressure which compels children to be sent to schools or for medical treatment. They might well be Jerusalem's "Dead End Kids" were it not for the social workers and places like those we visited. Some of these children have, after much persuasion, been taken from their parents for a couple of hours a day to a Community Council building. There they are taught the elementary rules of hygiene and social behavior. With the most primitive facilities they learn to play and relax in a structured environment. Then they go home and pass this information on to their mothers. They also get a wholesome meal, the kind they don't get at home.

One of the teachers at the girls school we visited in Nachalat Achim happened to be a friend who showed me around and told me some of the personal stories of these children. This one's parents were killed in the convoy to Jerusalem the other day, this one lives around the corner with eighteen brothers and sisters in one room, this one's father is a beggar and so on. Each one had a story. I had been so deceived by their happy faces and their hospitable smiles when they greeted me. This is the classroom for me, a far cry from the stuffy ivory tower of a University setup.

When I was interviewed by the Department Head in charge of the course I thought I owed it to her to be frank and admit at the outset that I didn't expect to do social work or, at least not practical case work, at the end of the course — which is scheduled to go on for six months. But, today as we passed the hovels where these people live and the institutions that cater to them, I almost yearned to rip off my coat, roll up my sleeves and lend my energies to the task.

It is now only 3:30 in the afternoon but I feel as if I've already put in a full day's work. I only started the course this morning; classes in this country begin at 8:00 A.M., which means you have to rise and shine two hours earlier. The Hebrew teacher, incidentally, is terrific — the kind of guy who happens to a classroom once in a long time — and, best of all, there are only six girls in the advanced class, so that it is practically individual instruction. And it's all FREE, including books.

After classes and the tour were over, at 11:00 A.M., I put in my five hours at work. Now, I've stopped at a cafe for some food and then I am homeward bound to *begin* the day's activities. It's amazing how much you can cram into twenty-four hours when you have to.

Love,<br>
*Zippy*

C O P Y

February 20, 1948

Hon.  Harry S.  Truman
The White House
Washington, D.C.

Dear Mr.  President;

On behalf of the Association of Parents of American Students in Palestine, I beg to transmit to you, enclosed herewith, a Memorandum which the Association has adopted, bearing on the security and welfare of our sons and daughters in Palestine.

As parents whose children are now exposed to the assaults of lawless violence, we beseech your sympathetic interest in the views and pleas set forth in our Memorandum.

Respectfully yours,
MRS. SAMUEL J. BOROWSKY
President

------------------------------------------------------------

ASSOCIATION OF PARENTS OF AMERICAN STUDENTS IN PALESTINE
314 West 91 Street
New York, 24, N.Y.
Telephone: TRafalgar 7-4885

RELEASE: FRIDAY, FEBRUARY 20, 1948

PARENTS OF AMERICAN STUDENTS IN PALESTINE SUBMIT MEMORANDUM

TO PRESIDENT TRUMAN AND SECRETARY MARSHALL

SUPPORTING SELF-DEFENSE MEASURES

- - - -

DECLARE THAT AMERICAN STUDENTS ARE OBJECTS OF "THREATS" BY U.S. CONSULATE IN JERUSALEM

------------------------------------------------------------

*Jerusalem*

*March 5, 1948*

Dearest Mother,

This morning I received by taxi service a big thick envelope and was thoroughly baffled. Even more so, when I opened it and noted the contents — an official-looking letter to the President of the United States and Secretary of State Marshall signed by *you*, plus a dramatic press release.

I read the enclosed Memorandum from the Association of Parents of American Students in Palestine carefully because I and all the other students here have waited a long time to get some official, clear and informative details about the phantom group that our parents have been referring to. It's interesting to note that you say the Association represents "500 students most of whom attend the Hebrew University in Jerusalem and the Hebrew Institute of Technology in Haifa." I hate to tell you, but most of them have already left.

After reading the letter and memo, I am rushing to answer you to let you know how very disturbed I am. Although I am trying very hard to be objective from this vantage point, the only explanation I can find for what you are doing is that your group is misguided and misinformed — troubled parents who are searching for an outlet for their tensions. Let me explain.

If your organization, as outlined in the memo, was founded for the purpose of protecting the basic human rights of American students in Palestine and safeguarding our civic status, then please note the following: any American student who has remained in Palestine despite the disturbances has remained here not because he can pursue his studies peacefully — he cannot — but rather because, as an American Jew, it is an opportunity to identify himself with the struggle of the Jewish people for survival and sovereignty.

If, however, his remaining here jeopardizes the word "American" in front of the word "Jew" in the eyes of his government, yet he continues to remain here, then it should be *perfectly clear* where his priorities lie at this moment.

What kind of dual nationalism is your Association offering us? On the one hand, you encourage us to continue to defend ourselves, "joining with all others who are similarly threatened," but on the other hand, you want to protect our passports for us and, if it comes to it, our citizenship.

We are not playing martyrs; we are being realists. It would be ridiculous for the American government to sanction any group, individually or collectively, joining the armed forces, legal or illegal, underground or aboveboard, of another country, even if the political policy of America favored intervention. America has a well-supported Army, Navy and Air Force, and doesn't need to operate through a student group to enforce a political or even military international agreement.

At best, by way of keeping her policy, as expressed in the United Nations vote on November 29th, America could assist in implementing the Partition Plan as it should be implemented. We have asked for no special protection and what we as individuals do should be of no official concern to the government. If our parents were smarter, and if they were *really* interested in protecting our civic status, they would permit these activities to go UNPUBLICIZED. You can't have it both ways.

We have received no "threats"; your information is erroneous. It was brought to the attention of the Consulate that American students, and particularly ex-servicemen who are receiving funds from the American government *in order to study,* are participating in defense activities. The Consulate was obviously forced to take some action and took the mildest one possible, a semi-threat. In the case of the Spanish Civil War, you recall, Americans who joined the forces were deprived of their citizenship.

We think the Consulate has played ball. It could have discontinued GI checks, it could have recalled our student

116

visas, it could have *enforced* its semi-threats. Be assured it is no feat to prove that students are actively participating in defense activities here; even a blind journalist could figure that out. To date, the Consulate has done none of these things.

I can understand the need for an organization of parents whose children are in a disturbed area of the world to get together to pool information, to discuss their mutual problems, to get to know each other socially, as their children do, and to be able to console each other at the right moment.

But, *any other purpose* negates what we are doing. Please understand that. The personal harm that can come to us, your children, as a result of bringing this matter to pressure point, bordering on investigation, is far greater than the political victory you may gain by pressuring President Truman and the State Department as you have been doing. We stand more to lose than to gain by that victory.

At best, the Consulate can *continue* to leave us alone. At worst, it can do a double-cross, as pulled by Austin on the UN Security Council, and actually make it very hot for us here. We don't trust the objectivity of the State Department, and bringing this matter to their attention to the point where they have to take action for public peace will only give them an excuse to take severe action against our civic status, which you are so anxious to preserve. As far as we are concerned at this moment, if our American citizenship denies us the right to defend ourselves in the face of attack, then who needs it? The last thing any of us want is to be forced to return to the States to *preserve* our citizenship.

I guess the whole matter was forcibly brought to the attention of the State Department by the profuse publicity about the death of Moshe Pearlstein, the American student killed here; who, incidentally, would have resented that publicity if he could have.

Let me say that, though I have expressed my own point of view, I think it may be safely taken as the point of view of the majority of the student group here, excluding those who have already left the scene and returned to the States or are about to do so.

I don't think I can add much more except to say that I hope you will take this letter very seriously. It may be that there are facts that we don't know about, but if there are we have a right to know what they are. So write. Don't forget that the majority of parents in your Association are probably trying their darndest, through every possible means, to get their kids home, and you may very well be assisting them. But, at the same time, you are making life very difficult for those of us who wish to remain.

Please reconsider this Association business.

Love,
*Zippy*


*Jerusalem*

*March 8, 1948*

Naomi Dear,

Our "Jewish Army" is really a hobo army. I went to the movies one night with some fellows from Tel Aviv, the elite soldiers (the Palmach) who shuttle back and forth, as armed guards, protecting the convoys between Jerusalem and the rest of the country. They showed up in the new Haganah "uniform": renovated British duds, but without stripes and bars or other signs of rank. The pants are skimpy and much too short, and so are the shirt sleeves, but it's a badge of honor to be seen wearing the "uniform" and they strutted around proudly. So did I.

They had tossed a coin to decide which of the two would take me out. I suggested, in the national interest, that we all go out together. The movie, Deanna Durbin in *Christmas Holiday*, was awful but the company was great.

In addition to many other miseries, Jerusalem has been hit by a terrible cold spell — positively the *coldest* winter I have ever had to live through. All the floors in the houses here are made of tiles, wonderfully cool in the summer but ice cold in the winter. The houses are all built of solid stone to withstand the searing summer heat, but the same insulation also does an excellent job of retaining the winter cold when there isn't any internal heating — and there usually isn't. It's an either/or situation.

Nearly all the windowpanes in the city are broken, so the sick joke of the week is that Jerusalem now has a new type of ventilation, thanks to the recurring bombings. The same source passed around the rumor that the blasting of Ben-Yehudah Street was perpetrated by the glaziers' union in an effort to increase employment. Personally, I think the building workers' union was in on it with them.

Love,
*Zippy*

*Jerusalem*

*March 14, 1948*

Dear Everybody,

The bombing of the Jewish Agency building has left us all numb with shock. It struck right at the nerve-center of

119

the *Yishuv*, at our most vital organ. And to think that the U.S. consular car, loaded with explosives and driven by an Arab driver who is well-known at the gate, should have been able so easily to penetrate this well-guarded building. And, that the American flag visible on the car should have been the chief accomplice. It's inconceivable, and yet it happened.

In the last few weeks, Jerusalem has had to face one devastating tragedy after another, each one overshadowing the other in intensity and violence. What next? . . . Where next?

Who can write?

Love,
*Zippy*

---

*Jerusalem*

*March 16, 1948*

Dear Everybody,

I awoke this morning to see SNOW on the treetops — pure white, feathery flakes. Jerusalem covered with snow is a sight for even an old time "snow-seer" like me to get excited about. But now, two hours later, the snow has melted and rain and hail are the order of the day. The streets are a mash of slush, inches deep, and no wonder, the snow having come after six days of heavy, steady rain and hail.

I am writing to you while sitting in a cafe, continental style. Actually, I came in to get out of the rain and felt silly just sitting, although everybody else does it for hours on end. For Jerusalemites, cafe sitting is almost as essential as food — and for some very sound reasons.

First of all, it's an ideal place to rendezvous with your friends. It's the perfect place to transact business, receive telephone calls and messages — all without having to pay rent: just the price of a cup of tea or ersatz coffee. It's a recognized "home away from home" where everyone knows you can be found at specific hours of the day. But most important, it's warmer in a cafe than in most homes in winter, and cooler than the streets in summer. So when you're thinking of private enterprise, that's the perfect business to go into.

I am at the Cafe Vienna, writing to background music provided by a young pianist who is pouring his heart into Chopin and looking around the room for inspiration. He just spotted me and is now rendering "Moonlight Sonata." It sounds so old-worldish to be serenaded this way, but frankly I'm finding it very relaxing. There is enough full-blooded tension in this city to entitle you to as much relaxing as you can find.

The popular greeting on the street these days is *Yiheyeh tov* (It'll be o.k.). I'm trying to be optimistic, but I don't see any end to this tension in sight. Maybe it's the rainy day mood, but our situation is, to say the least, disheartening.

Love,
*Zippy*

*Jerusalem*

*March 18, 1948*

Dearest Mother, Dad and Naomi,

As this letter will be mailed in New York by an American student, leaving while the going is still possible,

I'll try and write of the things I carefully never mentioned before, about me and the Haganah. But, please don't share this letter with anyone. It's *strictly confidential.*

When things got really serious in Jerusalem last month, marked by a chain of wanton and tragic anti-Jewish outrages committed in the heart of the city, five of us American girls were taken by the Haganah for a ten-day special course of *imunim* (training). Even those memorable days were sport for us. It was a good healthy feeling to live the life of a "safe" soldier, to dress sloppily and be bone-tired from physical work. And boy, did we get a workout. We learned to handle every small weapon that we might conceivably be called upon to use — pistols, rifles, sten guns — to take them apart blindfolded and shoot them instinctively or on order of "aim, fire."

We crawled till our bellies ached over the stony wadis and gorges and learned to run zig-zag, drop fast, crouch to conceal ourselves, camouflage, ambush, retreat — the works. We threw rocks till our arms were numb before being given dummy grenades. Basic Training like no American WAC ever had. Our instructors were men and they were merciless.

There were so many crazy-silly moments that I can never recapture, like when Rachie dropped "under fire" with her "can" sticking up in the air, a perfect target. Or the day we were told to "capture" a certain hill and to approach it without being noticed. We thought we would be smart and divided into two groups, planning to encircle the objective and strike simultaneously. The signal was a jackal cry — and darned if a jackal didn't howl at the crucial moment to louse up our act.

During those ten days, we were occasionally sent to do *tatzpit* (lookout or spyglassing) in the most unexpected places, the worst of which were water towers. Not such a ducky place to be on a cold windy day.

We had all kinds of crazy assignments after those ten days, the last of which I hope I never have again. Two nights a week, three of us would pack our blankets and trudge through the muddy wadis to report for patrol duty in one of the outlying workers' quarters overlooking "approachable" hills between us and two Arab villages. We each had to march around with a local Home Guard man for a four-hour stint, in silent search of signs of the enemy. The wakeful hours in between we would sleep on a cold army cot in somebody's barn or attic. Six o'clock in the morning would find us dragging ourselves home for a quick breakfast, a change and off to school or work.

We had crazy fun even at that. The first night we expected just the usual *shmirah* guard duties and then, suddenly, they slung at us British Army overcoats, false identity papers, rifle permits, rifles and ammunition — taking no chances in case a bona fide British patrol would actually appear. We split our sides laughing at the way we looked walking around in that getup. But, on the nights it rained, it wasn't funny at all.

The "dates" we got stuck with on these nocturnal patrols were men of singular valor and charm — all married and 4F [exempt from military service]. The guy I will never forget was the local doctor who cured me forever of frivolity in matters of security. I should mention that he was very hard of hearing. At about 3:00 A.M., the *bikoret* (inspection unit) came round and, to check on our alertness, crawled up the embankment, confronting us suddenly on the road. My partner didn't hear them and I almost shot them before realizing that it was a only a checkup. Then, the hot-shot inspector wanted to know why I hadn't asked for the *sismah* (password). He wouldn't believe me when I told him that I didn't know the password and that my partner couldn't possibly have heard it even if he *had* been told it. I almost got court-martialed.

But that's the past and thank goodness it's over. I no longer have to play at being soldier. At the moment, I have a wonderful assignment, which I can't tell you about, Top Secret. I've left out a host of fascinating experiences, but I think you've got an idea of what has been going on. As I reread what I wrote above, I realize how distortedly romantic and heroic it sounds. It's not that way at all.

The boys, of course, are doing other assignments, some more dangerous, some less. We keep track of each other like one big family. The whole country, in fact, is one big family IN TROUBLE.

Love,
*Zippy*

*Jerusalem*

*March 19, 1948*

Dearest All,

For the past few weeks, sandwiched in between all the other things I do, I've been acting as a kind of executive secretary and "Girl Friday" to Lou Kraft, my former boss at the Jewish Welfare Board in New York. He has come to Jerusalem to lay the groundwork for establishing the first Jewish Community Center (YM/YWHA) in the country. It's an enormous task to accomplish in a very short time and under exceedingly difficult circumstances. He simply came at the wrong time.

I am enjoying working with him immensely — helping him get to the right people, establish contacts, set up the Advisory Board, arrange meetings, etc. For me, in these times, keeping busy is the best thing I can do to take my mind off events over which I have no control. Also, it's just like old times to be fully occupied with something interesting and constructive, where I can leave my mark. The main problem I've been having is *taking care of Mr. Kraft.* He isn't used to dodging snipers and ducking his head down in dangerous areas: I'm practically playing nursemaid to keep him alive.

I have been working at top speed lately, including taking minutes at the Board meetings, and he has insisted that I accept renumeration. I know I've earned it but I still feel a little uncomfortable. After all, I did it because I wanted to. I'm also getting a million laughs out of it. For example, today, the Physical Education Committee met to look over the blueprints for sports facilities. Kraft was solemnly explaining where the pool would be, the locker rooms, and the other amenities. When he was all finished, the befuddled members of the Committee, mostly professors, started asking questions like the following:

"No *mikveh* (ritual bath)?"

"What's a bowling alley?"

"Men and ladies swimming together?" (Shocked look!)

"For what we need Turkish baths?"

"Why padlocks on the locks — what Jew would steal?"

"How can the pool be clean if no one wipes it clean?" This after a tedious explanation about circulating water, alum and chlorine, plus vacuum action.

"What kinda snack bar?— a Jew needs a full meal. We gotta have a restaurant!"

And so on, till I thought my mouth would explode from muscle strain trying not to smile. Tomorrow, the Cultural Committee will do its act.

I feel very fortunate to be involved in this project from its very inception. Years later, I know I'll feel proud to have had a part, however minor, in helping to launch the Community Center program, an entirely new concept here. Once it gets off the ground, it's bound to be a success.

Mr. Kraft has been very appreciative of my efforts, making me feel partly responsible for whatever is being accomplished. The man simply inspires devotion to the task. He introduces me to every important person he talks with as if I were President Truman's daughter instead of just an ad hoc assistant.

Before this came along, to try and get some normalcy into life, I took on free-lance editorial work — wherever and whenever I could find it. There are very few jobs available these days: everybody is retrenching and conserving resources. So, I consider that I have been fairly lucky. In addition to part-time work for the Jewish Agency Youth Department, I also worked briefly in another Agency department, subediting material translated from Arabic. The first few weeks, I managed to enjoy the work and to steer clear of internal intrigues. The Department Head seemed pleased with me, after four other Americans failed to meet his standards for accurate and fast work under pressure. Then, I discovered the reason for the steady turnover in the job: the English language. There are simply too many versions of it this side of the Atlantic: American-English, English-English and "P'English-English" (Palestinian English).

The Boss Man and I were at loggerheads much of the time. To give you some idea of the difficulty — he would insist that there was nothing wrong with using a phrase he had seen in the local English-language paper (which is the "P'English" Bible), even if it was *nobody's* version of English. Since there is obviously no way to win this kind of argument, I left him to find yet another victim. Anyhow, the very day I left, to my great good luck, Kraft called.

Have to close. Am sitting in a hotel lobby waiting for Kraft and I see he is heading this way . . . all smiles.

Love,
*Zippy*

*March 21, 1948*

Dearest Mother, Dad and Naomi,

Methinks Spring is around the corner. Today, the sun shone just as it says it is supposed to in all the travel books. I was beginning to think the propaganda about this being a tropical country was strictly Chamber of Commerce stuff.

And I didn't let the announcement of the U.S. shift in policy dampen my spirits either. After all we have been through, Warren Austin [the U.S. Delegate to the United Nations] has the gall to press the UN to abandon the Partition Plan in favor of a UN Trusteeship when the British Mandate ends on May 15th. At least, now we know where the State Department stands and we can go on with the fight without the illusion of support from our guardian angels.

I think that probably the Jews in America were more shocked and bewildered by this blitzkrieg than the *Yishuv*. Everybody here expected it, sooner or later: they have faith only in themselves, *Im ein ani li, mi li* (If I am not for myself, who will be for me)? It is a philosophy which says never count on anyone else for too much, for too long. Only family will stand by you in the hour of need. And, how right they are.

Nevertheless, they are worried that American Jews will despair, and that will be a more tragic a blow to the *Yishuv* than all the meandering policies of the State Department. We Americans here are being heckled with a full blast of the "I told you so" attitude, and we can't help feeling sheepish and ashamed of the way the American government has behaved.

No mail for the last few days — probably caused by the rerouting of mail through Cairo since TWA pulled out of the country. But, more important, there has been a temporary halt of convoys to and from the city. Even Mr. Kraft, who has top pull, is stuck in Jerusalem.

Love,
*Zippy*


*Jerusalem*

*March 23, 1948*

Dear Everybody,

Exhibit A: Life in Jerusalem. For three weeks I've been waiting for my grocer to save me an egg. I've got a ration card, but by the time I get to the store I'm registered at, which is in town, he's all sold out. Well, today he did it. With the utmost tenderness, he wrapped my egg in paper and, along with my ration of margarine, cheese and some other stuff, placed it gently on top of the parcel.

The entire bus ride I protected the egg vigilantly. Then bingo, right in front of the door, I missed a step and my three-and-a-half-*grush* treasure went flying. But I saved the day and part of the egg. Took the remains, added some powdered milk and powdered egg and scrambled up a delicious little dish. That should be the worst calamity to befall me.

In general, I splurged today — figured I needed a pick-me-up after the miserable winter. I spent almost two pounds (about ten dollars) on a lovely poplin sports shirt that I've had my eye on for a long time. I decided to get it while the getting was good; next week the store might be bombed out. Anyhow, the money I had earned was burning a hole in my pocket.

My social life has calmed down a bit since I showed one admirer the gate and another the door. Everybody plays for keeps here, so you've got a problem if you're not anxious for a relationship to develop. My favorite friends are out risking their lovely necks in not so lovely places, so now I have time to knit them sweaters and write them cheerful letters in fractured Hebrew.

Just heard that a *shayarah* (convoy) finally left.

So, if Kraft arrives safely, so will the letters I sent with him.

Love,
*Zippy*

*P.S.*

Forget the above. He was left behind. The seat was obviously needed for someone more important.

## Part Five

# Jerusalem Besieged

*March 29, 1948*

Dearest Each of You,

Jerusalem has been holding its breath for two days. A *shayarah* returning from Kfar Etzion was ambushed in the hills of Hebron by thousands of Arabs lying in wait all along the road. For thirty hours our boys fought for their lives before the British Army made any effort to get through to liberate them. Many of my friends and fellow students were trapped in the ambush.

To welcome some of them back, we had an old-fashioned shindig in my room tonight — Itzhak, Yossi and Dov were the guests of honor. In between mouthfuls of hot coffee, they gave us accounts of the battle which made our skin crawl. But despite the horrible ordeal and their frustration at having had to abandon precious vehicles and arms as loot to the Arabs, they are in good spirits.

After shaving, they actually looked like human beings, in contrast to the gorillas who had marched in an hour before. When they came to say good-bye two months ago, they had been told they would be gone for only a week. Who can make plans these days?

The people in this country are simply made of iron. It is unbelievable what they have to endure and how much they'll yet have to endure before this is over. I am not alone in my feeling of foreboding. Everyone senses that there are very difficult days ahead.

The Arab plan is not only to strangle our communication lines and destroy our outposts but to lay siege to the city and starve us into submission — with a little help from the British. The British don't believe for a moment that we'll be able to withstand an invasion by *seven Arab states* so the Mandatory policy calls for us to surrender the city to Abdullah, the King of Transjordan, when the Mandate ends on May 15th.

We aren't fooling ourselves. Jerusalem and its one hundred thousand Jews are in for it. Everyone knows there is no defending the city from a strategic point of view. Our only hope is international intervention in some form — a UN militia or some other neutral force. I can't believe the entire world would abandon the Holy City without making provisions for safeguarding the sacred places or trying to prevent an outright attack.

Any way you look at it, the picture is already grim. There have been no convoys out of the city for a week and, worse yet, none have arrived in Jerusalem. Food and water supplies are getting critically low and our worst nightmare, isolation from the Jewish State, may ensue. But, believe it or not, spirits are high. Everyday life goes on . . . with a minimum of the depressing atmosphere you would expect with everyone fully aware of what is in store.

I look at it this way. I am not a better or a worse person, a braver or a weaker person than anyone else here. As long as they can take it, I should be able to and, perhaps, then some. I like living in Palestine. I love Jerusalem. It is my home for now. I don't see why a person should pick up and leave his home because a dangerous madman has gone berserk next door. There is no running away. A couple of miles isn't going to make a difference. You'd have to run thousands of miles and keep on running the rest of your life.

Love,
*Zippy*

*March 30, 1948*

Dearest Mother, Dad and Naomi,

I met two American friends on the street today, both planning to leave Jerusalem. One has a teaching job lined up in Tel Aviv and the other is heading for a kibbutz. I thought of the comment making the rounds these days: "If any more people leave, this is going to be a ghost town." As for me, if it comes to leaving Jerusalem, I'd sooner take the next boat back to the States.

Maybe I am just a little bit envious of my friends. I'm *not* thinking of leaving but I wish to hell I could get out of the city for just a little while, maybe over Passover. But there's not the slightest chance. I am of "recruitment age" and I wouldn't even get permission to leave temporarily. I'm also very involved in commitments. Besides, there are priorities on the convoys. Hundreds of people, trying desperately to get to Tel Aviv, line up hopefuly every day at the Egged Bus Station, only to be turned away — *nothing* is moving out because *nothing* is coming in.

A convoy headed for Jerusalem generally sets out from Hulda or the outskirts of Tel Aviv with thirty, forty or fifty trucks laden with hundreds of sacks of flour, canned food, other staples and fruit — the city's needs for less than a day — accompanied by a couple of armed escorts to "protect" it. Burdened as they are, the trucks, which can't travel faster than about ten miles an hour, are perfect targets for a bloody massacre by the Arab bands that lay in wait.

If the convoy is in luck, maybe fifteen or so of the trucks will make it to Jerusalem. If they have been waylaid by roadblocks, most of the trucks will be knocked out of commission and block the way for the others, so the whole shebang becomes sitting ducks for the Arab attackers and the precious cargo is dislodged, scattered and looted. We've lost so many of these armored trucks — along with their drivers and Haganah protectors — that stocks are now almost nil. Rumor has it that the reason there are no convoys moving is because we have to wait till more "armored" cars can be made. Actually, they are regular buses and lorries with both sides of the driver's cabin fitted with a facing of thin metal sheets and a wedging of wood between the layers to save metal. They're nicknamed "sardine tins." The only "decoration" is a couple of slits for seeing and shooting.

In the meantime, while we are "girding our loins," the Arabs are busy setting up sturdier roadblocks and more effective ambushes — with the British standing by and not intervening. There is so much to tell you, but I cannot seem to find the serenity that it takes to write. Some day, soon. I hope.

I simply cannot believe that mail service out of the country will *really* be discontinued next month, as threatened.

Love,
*Zippy*


*Jerusalem*

*April 2, 1948*

Dearest Naomi,

We are not only physically oceans apart but also, mentally, worlds apart. So before writing to you, I always

find I need to switch back to my American wavelength —
which is so different from ours here. Not to speak of the
need to translate into English phrases you probably
wouldn't understand in either language.

The incongruity really hits me when I sit down to
write, as I am doing now — in a supposedly quiet corner of
a quiet cafe — and then BINGO, a barrage of gunplay strikes
up, sounding as if it were directly over my head, jolting me
into another sphere. People go right on reading the
newspaper, sipping their tea, knitting and not noticing. You
find that you too are not even hearing it, it is so familiar a
part of your everyday experience. Like the backfire from a
car or the party noise of ash cans banged by revelers on a
New Year's Eve binge. Well maybe I'm *not* hearing
anything, but my stomach hears and does a flip-flop.

I'm in a sober mood today, the kind that gets at you
every so often when the oppressive weather decides to play
ball with the miserable situation, and suddenly the whole
world and not just the sky above looks ominously cloudy.
Maybe what brought the mood on was the return of my
friends from the Kfar Etzion *shayarah* ambush.

In order to save lives — and the boys feel so guilty
about it — arms, trucks, everything had to be surrendered
to the British. The British, in turn, with the utmost
magnanimity, handed over those precious items to the
thousands of Arabs who had ambushed our men in the first
place — enough trucks and arms to supply and equip them
for ten more such ambushes. Jerusalem is elated about the
return of our boys but inconsolable at having lost
desperately needed armored cars, the only means of
contact with Tel Aviv and Jewish settlements in other parts
of the country — and at what price?

So whom shall we curse: The British, who are by now
deeply committed to their hostile policy? The UN, who

were to have implemented a fair solution to this messy situation? Or the American State Department, who are starting to play on both sides of the net? Perhaps ourselves, for being stupid enough to believe what we keep telling each other every day, *Yiheyeh tov.*

*Later . . .*

I had to stop. The shooting was getting closer and I went to find a quieter spot. Am now having lunch with a friend. The best place to get a meal these days is in a restaurant; the grocery stores certainly don't have anything to sell. We anticipate the arrival of a *shayarah* any day, but "any day" somehow doesn't come.

Am trying very hard to find something in the way of permanent work to dig my teeth into. Let's face it, another month or two and I'll be needing something to keep me going, not only financially, but also spiritually. Finding work isn't less difficult than finding food. Funny, yesterday the waiter in a cafe offered me a piece of cake. I had to laugh: bread is being rationed but the cafe somehow had managed to get flour for cake. What did Marie Antoinette say ? "No bread? Let them eat cake." All anyone ever talks about is FOOD.

I sense in your letters, Naomi, that you are thinking in terms of joining me in Palestine. Just to think about it is heartwarming but I'm afraid I have to tell you that this is no time to visit the Holy Land. Don't plan too heavily on it, you may have to change your plans not once but over and over again. You might even get so disgusted with having to constantly shift plans that you'll be discouraged from planning in this direction ever again.

No one can plan here from one second to the next. There is constant sniping and machine-gunning, and every day there are fresh casualties. People are being mowed down unsuspectingly, like mosquitoes. Believe me, Naomi, nothing would give me greater pleasure than to see you here — even for a brief visit — but I cannot honestly encourage you to come at this time. I hate to interfere in your personal affairs but be realistic and wait till I give you the go-ahead.

Love,
*Zippy*

*Jerusalem*

*April 7, 1948*

Dearest Mother, Dad and Naomi,

Yesterday, I enlisted in the "Army" (Haganah) full time. Until now, I have been doing my bit mostly in the evenings and on special assignments; for women it is still voluntary service. I simply decided that the moment to stand up and be counted had arrived.

When I presented myself at the mobilization center, I was directed to a fellow who looked at my name and asked if I came from Brooklyn. I said yes, and without another word, he proceeded to fill out the necessary forms. At the end of our interview, it dawned on me that he had mentioned Brooklyn before I had, so I asked if he had relatives there. It turned out that he was a scholar from Kibbutz Yavne and had heard of my distinguished Hebraist father. Thanks to your good reputation, I was saved hours of worry and waiting. The fellow really put himself out to be helpful to me. It's almost as difficult to enlist full time in the Haganah as it is to get permission to avoid getting "drafted."

The word "American" produces one of two reactions from people: either it creates a barrier or it makes you the center of attraction and wonder. For example, the doctor who gave me the physical examination discovered my humble origins when I failed to translate "chicken pox." He spent more time than was necessary taking my blood pressure and asking about hospitals in America.

As you probably have been reading in the papers, Jerusalem has had hard times of late. One *shayarah* managed to get through the other day, but in general, the situation is "snafu." The prospects of it improving are slimmer than the prospects of it getting much worse, so I am conserving the few cans I have left from the packages you sent. Believe me, I have begun to appreciate you in the full light of your worth, which tonight, for purely practical reasons, is FOOD.

There is absolutely NOTHING to be obtained in the food shops — especially if your ration card clearly states that you do not have three children, a husband and elderly parents to feed. The only place to get food is in the restaurants, where there isn't much — thin "potato" soup and mock "sausage," and no way of knowing what they are made of. After two days of stomach upsets I gave up eating out and have gone back to concocting. You'd be surprised what powdered milk and powdered eggs can do to revive each other when you slip in some foreign agent, a great deal of love, and mix well. Tonight, three of us had a feast, some noodles in powdered milk soup, a sardine salad and hot water with a pinch of coffee. So your packages have literally saved the day.

Please don't get the idea from what I have written that we are starving. It's just that there are temporary shortages. I guess it is inconceivable to expect you to understand that the package you sent which landed in Haifa cannot possibly be forwarded to me. A convoy to

Jerusalem carries only top priority things, essential food, arms and essential passengers. An inconsequential parcel for yours truly doesn't stand the slightest chance.

I had to laugh when I read what you wrote: "Can't you do anything about it?" Believe me, if I could, I would immediately be appointed Chief Administrator of Transportation for Jerusalem and Environs. A job I wouldn't relish.

The truth is that Mr. Kraft is still stuck here. Even the U.S. Consul can't get him out. There are about ten other VIP Americans who have plane and boat reservations and won't be able to make them. Said the Consul: "The British *could* get you out but I'm afraid your race is against you." Spit three times, curse and go back to pacing the floor trying to figure out an out.

Thank you, Mother dear, for your heart-to-heart advice to the lovelorn. But, please leave off that subject until further notice — it is the furthermost thing from my mind at the moment. Incidentally, I still have a last fifty-dollar reserve tucked away for doomsday. Till then, I'm sure I'll manage somehow. If you can, send me some money; if you can't, don't worry about it.

I discovered how not to worry in this country. So many unexpected things happen when you are not worrying about them and so many things you expect to happen don't happen at all when you worry over them that it is just a waste of time to worry at all. You can't win; best to take what comes and make the best of it.

Today was a misery of heat; spring has just begun. If this is spring, what will summer be like? The typical day in Jerusalem is brisk in the morning, hot at midday and chilly in the evening: you literally have to dress three times a day, like at a fancy hotel, or learn to shed and add. It's a real nuisance.

Have to stop; the electricity was just cut off and candles are at a premium too.

Love,
*Zippy*

*Jerusalem*

*April 11, 1948*

Dear Everybody,

The capture of Deir Yassin, a neighboring Arab village, by the *Etzel* the other night must have given the foreign correspondents a real field day. Rumors are circulating of indiscriminate killing of men, women and children. There's no way of knowing exactly what did happen but, if it was butchery, it took place *before* the Haganah was called in to help evacuate *Etzel* wounded. It is a conquest we are by no means proud of, though the extremist groups — *Etzel* and *Lechi* — are pretty pleased with themselves. It is outrageous and shameful and we are all horrified. That's the trouble with extremists: they never know when to stop. Not everything can be excused by calling it war.

I suppose there had to be some sort of retaliation for Deir Yassin — so it was the Arab shelling of Givat Shaul and Montefiore. As it happened, I was on duty in another area and not home at the time. When I did get home in the early hours, I found much less damage than I had been led to believe. A mortar shell had landed right on the main water tank next door, so we won't be having any water in our area for a few days.

Otherwise, everything is fine. We got picked on because we are right across the wadi from the village and a perfect target. But, as lightening rarely strikes twice in the same place, I expect our area will be quiet from now on.

Wool and nervous energy go well together. I've knitted myself what is called a "sandwich," a kind of slipover that meets front and back at the waist, olive green, with a beautiful intricate stripe stitch. I knit furiously during shelling attacks. At this rate, I should shortly be producing at factory speed — one a day.

Have to get back to my post.

Love,
*Zippy*

*Jerusalem*

---

*April 12, 1948*

Dearest All,

I noticed your letter in my box as I was leaving the house yesterday, in the dead of night, hugging my first aid kit, pack on back, for a twenty-four-hour duty stint. I slipped it into my pocket and made a mental note to read it later. Somehow, a kerosene lamp throwing shadows on a cobwebbed barn makes a letter from America seem rather romantic; even the words assume shadowy importance and hidden meanings.

This barn is Haganah headquarters for a string of makeshift bunkers connected by hand-dug trenches. I wanted to enjoy the letter in privacy and looked around to see who might be watching me. What I saw was the bare barn, filled wall-to-wall with a carpet of nineteen bodies wrapped in blankets, lying deathly still, sprawled out for an hour's rest on a cold cement floor. Off in a corner was

Naftali, making an awesome racket with his rhythmic snoring. This was one time I was glad of the earphones pressing on my ears. They muffled out the immediate sounds but magnified the impelling voices that would come any moment from the *emdot* (outposts) in the hills below.

I started to read the first paragraph hungrily but was halted abruptly. My earphones were sputtering. The guard was reporting the approach of our *mefaked* (officer in charge) returning from his inspection tour. He snapped out the password and lunged into the room, ordering me to immediately contact *emdot* one and four with an important instruction. My hands switched on the mike and I relayed the instruction.

It was a weird night. The orderlies brought the wounded to me, so all I had to do was sit tight, keep calm and figure out how to get the poor patient some proper medical attention if it was something I couldn't handle. Pot shots were being fired at us, the enemy presumably was advancing over the hills and my main worry that night was the pressing need to relieve myself and no privacy or place to do it.

I never did get to finish reading your letter until now.

Love,
*Zippy*

*Jerusalem*

*April 14, 1948*

Dearest Mother, Dad and Naomi,

Where to begin and how to say it? It is more or less quiet for a day or so and you start to breathe freely, look up at the sun, glad it is shining and happy that the world is existing — and then BANG.

The horrible Hadassah convoy massacre. The whole city is in mourning. So many friends, so many doctors, nurses, patients, university scientists, administrative staff, such a heavy loss, so damn much of everything.

The funeral is this afternoon — a mass funeral. All of Jerusalem is walking around asking itself: "Is there no end to it?" A couple of hours later the sun is still shining and you are kept so busy with the things that you have to do that you seem to forget — forget until the next tragedy. And so it goes.

I haven't seen the entire death list yet. Some seventy people, among them Dr. Yassky, the head of the hospital, plus scores of wounded. The convoy was attempting to reach Hadassah Hospital on Mount Scopus when they were ambushed passing through Sheikh Jarrah. Only a few people were killed outright; the rest could have been saved if the British Army convoy, which people claim to have seen less than a hundred yards away, had responded to their call for help. Instead, it continued on its merry way, leaving our wounded lying helpless in immobilized ambulances so that the Arabs could come in for the kill.

Forgive me for being so downhearted. But, God, you do get depressed in the moments when you have time to think — thank goodness that's not very often. Aside from the physical inconveniences — lack of water, food, electricity, mail, security in any form — the constant awareness of the political situation and the oppressive world picture are enough in themselves. And, when in a free moment you take stock, the result is devastating. The "comforting" thought is that it could be much worse than it is and no doubt will be before long.

Another "comforting" thought: I'm glad I'm not in America. I think I'd go batty if I had returned to the States with those who left and had to read in the papers about what was happening here. No frustration on that score. For once, both my conscience and I are precisely in the right place.

The British Mandatory government is intent on leaving the country in chaos. They've announced that as of April 30th *all* postal services — airmail, cables, phones, local and foreign — will be discontinued.

If they do pull out, the General Post Office will remain right in the heart of the Arab section. Even today, I imperil my life every time I go there to get your packages. Not only that, but I have to pay as much as two or three pounds for taxes, transportation, etc., no matter what you have prepaid on it. This is not America.

Air Freight is even more of a headache; you don't deal with the Post Office but with an agent, who also takes an exorbitant sum for his fees and trouble and is also in an inaccessible place. So, though I would love to have your packages, forget it. Times have changed.

Love,
*Zippy*

*Jerusalem*

*April 18, 1948*

Dearest Mother, Dad and Naomi,

Hallelujah. A convoy! I don't know which is more exciting: the fact that a convoy finally got through at dawn yesterday with supplies for Passover or that with it came a slew of friends, including Yehudah and Ami, all alive and well. Last night was certainly cause for celebration, but in the midst of the revelry the shooting started again and we had to head for shelter.

The convoy was enormous — over two hundred lorries — and not a shot fired at it. For two weeks the Palmach has been carrying out an intensive operation, battling every inch of the way with the Arabs for control of the hilly territory dominated by the Castel fortification. My friends were in the thick of this all-out effort to open the road for our convoys. [It was code-named "Operation Nachshon" after the fellow who was the first to plunge into the Red Sea, causing it to part.] Dare we hope that this is the beginning of clear traffic?

For the first time in months life is looking a little brighter. It started when people ran into the streets to greet the convoy, and the first thing they saw were the heart-warming words, "If I forget thee, oh Jerusalem," chalked on the lead lorries.

Incidentally, these Sabras are strong on *chutzpah*. This morning I was supposed to have been at my first aid post at 6:00 A.M., but without asking me, Yehudah went to my supervisor — he knew him because he had previously been his commander — and got me off the day's roster so that I would have no choice but to spend my free time with him. He's only going to be in town for a week; the problem is that *all* my friends are only going to be in town for a week.

When I mentioned to him that I had a noontime appointment about work with someone in the Education Department, he just tagged along; it turned out that the "someone" was his uncle. Naturally, I got preferential treatment. It's called *Protectzia*.

I can't really object to the other thing that Yehudah has arranged without asking me. He's invited me to his family Seder. I was all set to decline gracefully but it seems

147

"Mama" has already been informed about the "guest from America" and I can't get out of it now.

Love,<br>Zippy

Jerusalem

---

April 22, 1948

Dearest All,

Haifa is in our hands. A whole town captured by the Haganah, not just a village or a stronghold. Jerusalem is bursting with joy. Yesterday, the British moved out of Haifa officially in accordance with their evacuation plan and we took over. No one can understand how it happened that they didn't just hand it over to the Arabs before we could get into action.

Everywhere else in the country, we are told, the Arabs are attacking in full force on all fronts. We aren't doing so great in Jerusalem either. A plan to liberate the Jewish Quarter of the Old City nearly succeeded but didn't.

Anyhow, everyone has food for the holidays, the weather is glorious and I have just been whistled at approvingly by the guy across the hall. It's good for the morale when someone notices I'm really a girl; I get tired of being just "one of the boys" all the time. Had a great day today cleaning up my room, moving around the furniture to get a new look and thinking about unimportant things like what I will wear to Seder.

In a way, I am lucky, not having to wait in the long lines for the meager rations of meat and fish that are being distributed to heads of families. But, we did get a small ration of potatoes, margarine and wine and, with all the stuff I've been saving from packages you've sent, I should be fairly well-stocked for the entire holiday. Things are more organized since the Emergency Committee took over. It's headed by Dov Joseph, a former Canadian lawyer, who is scrupulously fair about distributing our almost nonexistent reserves.

*Later . . .*

Had to stop writing. WATER was suddenly turned on for an hour. Rushed to wash my hair, bathe and do some laundry. Am getting very resourceful at conserving water — it is amazing how inventive you can be when you have to stretch a bottle of water for food, wash, laundry and a hundred other uses before you slop it into its final resting place, the toilet.

Hope you have a Happy holiday.

Love,
*Zippy*

## *Jerusalem*

### *April 24, 1948*

Dearest Mother, Dad and Naomi,

I must tell you how I spent Seder night in besieged Jerusalem.

It was a wonderful evening, a huge full moon floating in a bathtub of blue, with little sparklers of stars hovering close by. The Mediterranean sky defies description. It's even more brilliantly star-studded than a summer night in Vermont. And at eye level, all this beauty is silhouetted against stark earthy rock and rugged hills.

We walked to town, marveling at the unexpected quiet. Not a shot to be heard the whole way. We were in high spirits, stopped off to bid *Chag sameach* (Happy holiday) to mutual friends, sang loudly and waved to people sitting on their balconies enjoying the quiet and waiting for Seder guests. Everybody has guests this year. There are about a hundred drivers in town who brought the last convoy to Jerusalem, stranded away from their families, and of course hundreds of soldiers far from home.

Seder night falling on a Friday eve in Jerusalem is doubly special. The holiday atmosphere is in the very air. The only sign of the times was a thick security guard surrounding the Chief Rabbi's home in Rehaviah, a block away from where we were headed: Yehudah's family Seder at an uncle's house.

As we mounted the stairs, I was a little apprehensive at the prospect of meeting three generations of relatives, but my fears were allayed in no time. I discovered that I knew the sister from my first aid course, and her husband and I had once done patrol duty together. There were several other guests and, reigning over all, was a regal grandmother, whose withered hand we all had to formally kiss following *Kiddush* over the wine. There is a 105–year-old great-grandmother too, but she was at Seder elsewhere because of the transportation difficulties.

The family is Sephardic in origin so, although the *Haggadah* was read in Hebrew, the important passages were reread in Ladino for the benefit of the grandmother, with everyone at the table taking turns reading, as we do at home. Whenever the conversation lapsed into Ladino, the children — little chauvinists — were genuinely upset and demanded that only Hebrew be spoken.

As I was a special guest, they provided me with a *Haggadah* which had an English translation. And, because they probably thought American Jews have no traditional background, they took great pains and derived much pleasure from giving me instructions on what to do and how to do it. I didn't have the heart to tell them that I knew a thing or two about Passover Seders.

The herbs were truly bitter, plucked from the fields, like the greens we now eat with our daily fare. The *charoset* tasted every bit like the Egyptian bricks it was supposed to represent, although in these times there's no way of knowing what it was made of. In essence, the Seder ceremony was the same as it is all over the world wherever Jews congregate.

Only one custom was strikingly different. I rather liked it. Instead of the *afikoman* being placed between two pillows, as we do, it was placed in a napkin, with its ends tied in a knot. [The *afikoman* is the half piece of matzah that is wrapped in a napkin and set aside until the end of the meal when, having been "stolen" by one of the children present, it is redeemed for a present.] Then the matzah bundle was passed to each one at the table, who in turn slung it over a shoulder and held it there for a bit, symbolizing the way the Jews must have carried their belongings out of Egyptian bondage. When it came to one of the children, it miraculously disappeared and was only forfeited against the promise of a book.

A five-year-old boy, the youngest in the family, in lispy Hebrew that seems to characterize the speech of most Sabra children, didn't merely *recite* the traditional four questions but *asked* them, in the most natural way, as if inquiring, "Why is this night different from all other nights?" His hands clasped around his knees, his head tilted to one side, as if he really didn't understand and wanted to be told why a Seder in besieged Jerusalem was different from any other.

Despite the terrible food shortage, a meal of sorts was served, simple but plentiful, with *kneidlach* [matzah balls] made from something that tasted like nuts. When the singing started it was really joyful. I was asked to sing the melodies I knew, which were very different from theirs. But, judging by the way they all beamed, my performance must have been enjoyable and interesting for them.

We had to leave early because of the long walk home, but not before saying formal good-byes and kissing — you guessed it — Grandma's paw with great ceremony.

We took a shortcut home to be out of the firing line, from the Generali Building (the British Mandatory government office compound) and through the crowded Mahaneh Yehudah area, a very religious community. At one house we saw by the flickering candlelight in the window a large family group huddled around the holiday table, the youngsters' earlocks dangling on the cloth, all singing with Hasidic fervor, transported with joy. Their singing had a haunting quality I cannot convey. Every corner of the deserted cobblestone alley reverberated with the sound of it, echoed and reechoed from every house. We hit the open road near Romema and broke into song ourselves, joined by the guards we passed at the various checkposts and roadblocks en route.

This morning, Alizah and I made a matzah omelette from our special Passover ration of one egg each.

It's unnaturally quiet today. I hope it isn't the quiet before the storm. Please plague me with letters. After April 30th, when the British will discontinue all postal services, there is no way of knowing what will be . . .

Happy holiday,
Love,
*Zippy*

— NOTE —————————————————————————————

*The cease-fires referred to constantly on the pages that follow were a series of on-again, off-again attempts at mediation by the UN and various official bodies, resulting in several intermittent cease-fire arrangements which lasted only a day or so before being broken.*

*Ultimately, there were two major cease-fire agreements: the first (starting June 10th) sustained for almost a month, and the second (starting July 18th) which lasted until a truce was negotiated six months later.*

*Jerusalem*

*May 9, 1948*

Dearest Family,

It is horribly, ominously quiet today, the first day of the cease-fire . . .

For me, this cease-fire is totally traumatic. A complete contrast, after just returning from a week of first aid duty in Deir Yassin, the Arab village which the Haganah took over after *Etzel* and the Stern Gang had captured it in a very messy operation. The combination of quiet and inactivity even for one day screams with a normalcy I haven't quite acclimated to.

Each of the seven days in last week fused into one another with such intensity and force that the hours were pressed into moments, flooding each other with activity, with flashes of thoughts and contrasts of emotion, terrifying to contemplate because they assail me with such clarity and constancy, even now a week later. A million impressions lined up, a list I have since lost. I wanted so to write it down, to pour it out, to catch it and preserve it in words. I so needed an outlet, a release from the pent-up tensions. It was such a soul-wrenching confrontation.

Only a week before I came to Deir Yassin, over two hundred Arabs, including Iraqi irregulars, but also innocent men, women, children, dogs and mules, had been killed there, wiped away with a callousness that clogs the mind with its incredibility.

I was trying desperately not to think about anything the bright, beautiful day that I crossed the fields and the wadi to present my credentials to the guard at the stone quarry — most of the villagers had been stone hewers. I climbed up the spiral road, past the roofless, black-burned, blood-spurted houses to the topmost house, humming, from some inner compulsion to rev up my spirits, fearful of what I would find ahead.

The earth was brittle with rocks and burnt dust. It crunched under my feet, patterned itself into a footprint for a short moment and then nudged by a soft wind dispersed itself in all directions. The rocks scraped against the soles of my sandals, burning and bruising my feet. I slowed my pace.

From the distance, the cluster of dome-shaped, dumb-struck houses looked deserted, like silent tombstones esthetically scattered over a gently sloping cemetery . . . a mass graveyard. As I entered the village, as if summoned by some unseen signal, swarms of dusty men appeared from the skeleton buildings, dragging out household items and articles of clothing. Like bustling, burdened ants our soldiers hurried, the barrels of their guns squinting in the sunlight. They hurried to eradicate the symbols of the dead, the remnants of things that no longer had owners, to bury them, burn them, to rid their noses of the smell, their eyes of the sight and their hearts of the knowledge. They worked swiftly, silently, efficiently, deliberately.

At closer range, the tombstone buildings looked like a huge piece of Swiss cheese, dotted with various-sized holes that bore the pressure of hot, furious lead and the mark of shattering precision. The fragments of jagged window-panes hung askew in their skeleton-like frames; the cement-bagged barricades were collapsed in confusion.

As the road mounted, the air thickened with dust and an overpowering stench. Everywhere, colorful shreds of clothing fluttered in the dry breeze and pots and pans rocked futilely on the porches of abandoned houses. At the crest of the hill, the houses were relatively unscathed, untouched by the insult of bullets. Sheltered and remote, they overlooked the cowering hushed village with stark dignity.

All these mixed feelings and thoughts were abruptly checked as I entered the topmost house, the *mateh*, Haganah HQ — formerly the home of the Mukhtar (the Mayor). A thick embroidered tapestry draped over a table and an oversized red plush, wood-carved, high-backed chair obstructed a first full view of my new commander. I introduced myself: the nurse assigned to set up an infirmary and first aid post. He flashed a broad smile which flooded his handsome face with warmth. The message was clear. Relax. Don't be afraid. We've got a dirty job to do and a difficult time ahead. Get on with it and do the best you can. Welcome!

---

— *NOTE*

*On May 14, 1948, the establishment of the State of Israel was proclaimed in a moving ceremony at the Tel*

*Aviv Museum Hall. Light years away in Jerusalem,
which was not yet linked to the State, we never even
heard the broadcast because our electricity was
completely cut off.*

*Isolated as we were, nevertheless, we shared the
wondrous sense of fulfillment that all the House of
Israel felt that day.*

*I couldn't grasp it. I never thought I'd live to see a
Jewish State. The war would now go into high gear but,
at least, we would be masters of our own fate, in our own
land.*

*Stuck in an Arab village, with no writing paper
available, I scrawled the letters that follow on the reverse
side of order forms for quarry products belonging to a
stone crusher. The letterhead bore the name Haj Assad
Radwan. To create a writing pad, I stitched the pages
together with sewing thread.*

## Jerusalem

### May 15, 1948

Dearest Family,

It's the most incongruous and inexplicable feeling. I'm
sitting on the Mukhtar's bed in Haganah headquarters in
Deir Yassin and, along with our soldiers, listening all hearts
and ears to the proceedings at the UN Security Council
over a broken down battery radio — trying to find out who
will recognize our new State. The room is lit only by a small
kerosene lamp which throws eerie shadows on the wall and
plays havoc with the imagination. The voices fade in and
out, the static is maddening and it is hard to hear who is
speaking. At the moment, the Representative from Canada
is saying something stupid — it's difficult to catch more

than a word here or there — so I'll use his time to write a few words . . . which may never reach you.

Awareness of the full impact of the significance of this day has been somewhat lost to me in the immensity of rapidly developing events that have gripped Jerusalem. The British are actually leaving. We are fighting desperately to take over their strongholds before the Arabs do. For the last three days we have been on full alert and this is Zero Hour.

We are waiting impatiently for the return of the contingents of boys dispatched for today's engagements. Many dear friends are among them. Somehow, that seems more important to me than what the "Gentleman from Canada" is jabbering about — or is it the Egyptian now?

Egypt. Oh, yes. They are invading rapidly to assure "peace and order."

The faces around me relaxed a bit after hearing that America had recognized *our State*. I feel a bit redeemed. Everyone in the room pivoted around to look at me as if I had had something to do with the decision.

What am I doing here? I'm in charge of the first aid post which has been whitened and brightened for the gruesome business anticipated. The stretcher-bearers are squatting nearby. One of them, a boy with dark curly hair, is resting his head against my knees and looking past the ceiling to the future. Everything we have is ready — blankets, bandages, a bit of cognac; ready for . . . we don't know what. This afternoon, it was heavy mortar fire, twenty-five pounders or more. Tonight, it may be air bombardment.

When I first donned these overalls and learned to sleep with my boots on and one ear open, I felt like a character out of a Hemingway novel, a partisan: one girl for every hundred men. Now, I'm into the role completely. I do the

157

most terrible things without agonizing over them, like rummaging, not maliciously but out of necessity, in the rubble of an Arab hut looking for a bed, a table or whatever else can be scrubbed up and made use of in my makeshift infirmary. One ceases to think of the dead Arabs whose houses and belongings we are utilizing, but rather of the dead Jews — the friends, the fathers.

We are completely cut off. No mail service out of Jerusalem, but writing eases the anxiety of waiting and worrying. How many of our boys will make it back tonight?

I wish we could know what is going on. So close and so far from the overall picture . . .

*Jerusalem*

*May 16, 1948*

Hello Again,

Day Two of the THE STATE OF ISRAEL. Had to abandon writing temporarily for more pressing business. It's a beautiful day, plenty of sunshine, flies and shooting.

My only American compatriot here, Herbert, dug up a pair of shorts for me to wear. He says the boys need it for their morale and never mind if Florence Nightingale never wore shorts. What an outfit for duty.

Everyone gets such a kick out of the fact that there are Americans in their midst. I'm actually the first American GIRL most of these men have ever seen. In fact, I'm becoming a legend here. They call me "Tzippy HaAmerica'it" (Zippy the American).

There are about three hundred men at this base from all over the world but only two of us from the U.S.

Anyhow, what we lack in numbers, we both make up for in other ways. For one thing, we are doing a fine job of public relations, having constantly to improvise with practically nothing at hand. Herbert set up a first-class cafeteria in the mess and is demonstrating what American efficiency is all about. And I'm doing my best in the two fields at my disposal, woman and nurse. The sweetheart of the camp and all that. I also set up a very cozy infirmary, thanks to super resourcefulness.

*Later . . .*

Pardon the inconsistencies, but I'm constantly being interrupted by minor emergencies — a scorpion bite, an attack of appendicitis, infections, a misdirected bullet, all in a day's work. In between, I serve sulphur tablets and good cheer, the best part of the job.

Our soldiers are like no others I've ever seen. They don't have much to fight with besides guts and determination. No swagger, spit or polish. No drinking, no shirking. Doing the dirtiest jobs, they sing and joke, even in the fiercest moments, and never with a "here today and gone tomorrow" attitude. Tomorrow is what it's all about.

I am grateful to be here with them. I have become one of them more than ever now.

* * *

Don't part with this envelope if you ever receive it. The stamps were issued for *five days only* prior to the declaration of the State and were available only in Jerusalem. They'll probably be valuable to stamp collectors in a couple of years. [It shows the map of Partitioned Palestine with the words "Jewish State" and *"Doar"* (Post).]

*May 20, 1948*

Dearest Family,

Pardon me while I make history. This is the first typewriter that ever kicked its keys in an Arab village or, at least, in this one. And what's more, it has the "distinction" of having been pecked at formerly by the British High Commissioner's personal secretary, or so I am told. Spoils of war, if you please. It's an overseas Underwood given to me for safekeeping by Moshe, who was in the occupying party at "Bevingrad," until his unit returns to us — that is if I'm still here. The boys tell me that the takeover at "Bevingrad" was a surprise walkaway. Not a shot fired. The British moved out, we moved in.

There must be a more expressive word than incongruous — which I can't think of — that could begin to describe this period and the way it impresses me. I get the strong urge to pinch myself several times a day . . .

Sometimes, in the middle of the night when mosquitoes are plaguing me and the incessant deafening sounds of cannon, mortar and machine gun fire, raining death and destruction on the Holy City, explode the possibility of sleep . . .

Sometimes, first thing in the morning, when I hop out of what was formerly "Fatima's" bed, grab a towel, reach for a jug of water, and do my daily dozens in a primitive outhouse . . .

Sometimes, in the makeshift mess, when the men, bleary-eyed and unshaven, have just returned from an engagement and have been without food or sleep for a day or more, yet remember to pass me my portion first or the first cigarette we have gotten in a week; or, more precious, the first smile they can summon . . .

Sometimes, the incongruity hits me as I am bandaging a wound, washing a patient, scouring the stone floor, reassuring a frightened soldier or trying to cheer up the bedridden because I have hardly anything else with which to treat them . . .

Sometimes, in the evenings as we sit around in groups singing at the top of our lungs or being deathly still and listening, depending on the alert . . .

Sometimes, I am aware of it in the bright sunshine, standing on a stone ledge above a sloping terrace, washing used bandages in a big Arab soup pot or rolling them carefully for reuse. I look out across the hills of Jerusalem, at the patches of green peeking through red rooftops, domes and spires and I am drunk in its beauty . . .

But mostly, the great gap hits me when I think of me here and of you in America. What a long way I've come. Has it been only seven months? It feels more like seven lifetimes. And it's not over yet . . .

*Jerusalem*

*May 23, 1948*

Dearest All of You,

No mail out of the country but I'm writing just for the hell of it. Had an hour off today so I thought I'd go back to the house for a breather, a change of underwear and some writing paper and to try to find out about my close friends and what is going on in other parts of the city and the rest of the country.

All that lies between this Arab village and Kiryat Moshe, where I live, is a rugged stretch of God's stony earth which was recently converted into an emergency landing field for a small piper plane which, when it's serviceable, ferries urgent communiqués and essential VIPs to and from Jerusalem. The airstrip is a constant target for mortar fire from Nebi Samwil, the highest spot in Jerusalem.

Today seemed quiet, so I braved it. The walk there was uneventful. But just my luck to be caught on the way back in the open field, completely exposed during a full-scale shelling session. For extra protection, I said a fast *"Shema Yisrael"* (the appropriate prayer for departing this world), flopped on my belly, dug my teeth and elbows into the ground, covered my head with my knapsack and squirmed forward as fast as I dared. Half an hour later it was over. I picked up some shrapnel for souvenirs and did a fast crouch run back to the base.

The sentries were blubbering all over me. Was I all right? Why had I gone alone? Why had I gone at all? Go explain that I needed desperately to make contact with civilization, to breathe some fresh air beyond this haunted Arab village, even if only for a brief moment. Even at a bit of a risk.

It was stupid of course. Yesterday was one of the worst days yet, ghastly, terrifying. My eardrums are bursting from the constant pounding of artillery. Worst of all is the psychological insecurity. Everyone in town, including women and children, is feverishly busy building barricades, digging trenches and filling sandbags. There are few shelters and no defenses and a terrible awareness that every shell is a hit-or-miss affair, with no rhyme or reason directing it. At least, here on the outskirts of town we know, more or less, the direction from which the firing is coming — Nebi Samwil — and, occasionally, can answer back.

Heard that the UN has appointed Count Folke Bernadotte to mediate this mess. Maybe he'll have some luck arranging a cease-fire.

The Jews in the Old City can't hold out much longer. Trapped inside the ancient walls, they are a besieged quarter within a besieged city and every attempt to break through to them has so far failed . . .

*Jerusalem*

*May 26, 1948*

Dearest Ones,

Last night was a trying and terrifying night — the night before a proposed cease-fire was to go into effect. We knew the Arabs planned to push as far forward as possible and we, too, intended to make the most of it.

We slept with our boots on, the stretchers lined up for action; but we didn't sleep. Airplanes were soaring overhead, the air was thick with whining shells, the incessant pounding of thundering blasts, ear-splitting explosions. My teeth rattled every time the building shook.

My infirmary was almost empty of patients, but swarming with mosquitoes and oppressive heat. It was unbearable. Ignoring the hazard, I curled up on a stretcher outside the door and watched the moon-filled sky lit up with fire and fury. For some strange reason, the fear in my heart melted to a peacefulness I hadn't known before. I was no longer afraid. Maybe I had squared myself with my Maker; He would have to decide if I was needed more down here or up there.

Days ago, I read through the booklet distributed to us on "Mastering Fear" and discarded it. The only way for me to deal with fear is to ignore it and face every frightening moment with as much resolution as I can muster. Keeping busy helps too.

By 6:00 this morning the din lulled to an occasional blast and I dozed off for a bit only to be wakened by a winking sun. Then, to the routine of the day . . .

I keep beginning letters, knowing I won't be able to finish them, impelled by the need to share words, to somehow be close to you, to pour out my heart. This last month, when all contact with the world outside Jerusalem has been cut off, I worried, knowing how much you must be worried. I am helpless to assure you that I am well and unscathed — which is no mean feat these days — and in good spirits.

I think I have changed in many ways from the girl you kissed good-bye that day at the pier. I've seen so much of life and death, it would be impossible not to have been affected. How have I changed? Well, I sense a flexibility in me that I wouldn't have admitted to before and a measure of self-discipline and restraint that is new to my spontaneous, rebellious spirit. Nursing, perhaps, released a natural warmth, the kind of humanness that is stifled and repressed in the New York jungle.

Blood, gushing freely in my hands, no longer fills me with fear and panic, but becomes a message requiring decisive and deft action. And you know that, perhaps, you have saved a man's life. I have caressed so many sweated brows, smiled at so many harassed faces and seen the magic work. I am convinced that care and compassion do the job even where medicine fails, or, in this case, isn't available.

My hand is flowing over the pages, but it is my heart that is really pouring itself out . . . sitting by kerosene lamp, dreaming of faraway places, listening to the whistle of mortar shells, the explosion of cannon shots pounding at us relentlessly. How much more of this can we take?

*Jerusalem*

*June 6, 1948*

Dearest Family,

Jerusalem is in mourning since the Jews in the Old City surrendered to the Arab Legionnaires. I suppose it had to come but it was a terrible blow. In a way, it has strengthened our resolve to hold out, no matter what.

There is constant talk of cease-fire but nobody has much faith in it. Nothing ever comes of it. Oddly enough, there are people, mostly the extremist groups, who think it would be a mistake to agree to cease-fire right now while we are getting the upper hand in the rest of the country; everywhere, that is, except Jerusalem. I think we desperately need the rest and respite and a chance to prepare for the next round.

The other night — I guess it was two or three days ago; I can't keep track of the passage of time — about midnight, I was sitting quietly in the infirmary with the kerosene lamp low watching the smoke rise and disappear into the heat of the room when, suddenly, I heard a gentle knock on the shutter and a friendly voice saying:

"I've got something for you. Orders were to deliver it in person."

In the darkness I couldn't see who it was but I was handed three letters *from America*. Not one or two, but THREE, dated early May — only a month ago. I wasn't sure whether to just have a good cry or turn up the lamp and read them.

Fate decided for me. The alert was sounded and I was called out to attend to someone who had accidentally stepped on one of our mines. The letters were shoved into my overalls pocket and remained there until early dawn when I tenderly took them out one by one to read, to reread and devour.

I had resigned myself to the fact that no mail would be coming through and not to expect any. But, of course, I forgot that outside of Jerusalem the State is beginning to function, taking over public services formerly run by the British. From Tel Aviv, apparently, there is mail moving in and out of the country; the problem is to get it to Tel Aviv. That's like going to the moon. I have no idea how these letters reached me. I can only be grateful . . .

Groping for a piece of paper every free moment to write a letter that isn't going anywhere is weird, but not half as uncanny as the urge that impels me to keep writing so as to have letters ready if ever I get a chance to send them . . .

*Jerusalem*

*June 8, 1948*

Dear Everybody,

My friend Yehudah pitched up to assure me that, despite persistent rumors to the contrary, he is alive and well. He's contrived a plan to get my mail to you that makes the old Pony Express laughable. It goes something like this:

I'm to give it to a mutual friend who will get it to him from which point he'll pass it on to another mutual pal of ours who in turn will transfer it to a friend in Tel Aviv for stamping and mailing.

Of course, this relay operation is as unreliable as life itself here, but I'll take the chance just the same.

He told me that Carmi and Judah Stampfer are both machine-gunners in his outfit, under his command, and brought me notes from each of them. Says they are doing a wonderful job, especially Carmi who is the rage of the Palmach, but better not pass this on to his family. Aryeh Fishman was wounded in the leg, not seriously. He's recuperating at the moment. He was lucky. He walks. He laughs. He's well. From all reports, Rachie, both Morties, Alizah, Donnie, Skippy and Ezra are all fine. Of course, I don't see them but I have constant reports from our boys who meet them in engagements — my soldier pals are trained to ask about Americans anywhere they go.

I have no words to describe what has come to pass in Jerusalem in the last few weeks. All I can do is send fragments of letters, written in various moods at odd moments on scraps of paper, scribblings, written more to myself than to you. Maybe they will give you some idea of what's been happening, at least to me.

If this letter ever reaches you, it'll be *the first to come out of besieged Jerusalem.* So rush to the phone and call up the families of all the friends mentioned here and give them the good news about their kids. They'll bless you for it.

I forgot to mention, I'm feeling fine and all in one piece.

\* \* \*

Still no word of a cease-fire . . . this can't continue much longer . . . I don't know how we will hold out . . . God, it is awful. Without letup. Can't you put some pressure on the State Department to do something about a cease-fire?

Must finish. Our boys are going out any minute . . . just waiting for my letter. The first stage of the relay arrangement.

*Zippy*

The Ben-Yehudah Street bombing, February 1948, where the author administered first aid for the first time (*E. Knoller*).

A major event during the siege of Jerusalem in 1948: the arrival of the kerosene delivery man (*courtesy of Ray Noam*).

A convoy bringing critically needed food and other supplies to besieged Jerusalem (*courtesy of the Haganah Archives*).

Temporary ID card issued by *Chen*, the Women's Corps of the new Israel Defense Forces.

The author in front of the Haganah first aid station at Deir Yassin during a cease-fire.

Part Six

# Finally a Cease-Fire

Dear All of You,

A small convoy of jeeps (with Palmach friends) bearing blessed arms, ammunition and food came via the hills the other night, using a secret route that bypasses Latrun, where the main battle for the road is going on. They're headed back for a reload — the first jeep transport out of Jerusalem. They have a much better chance of getting through than armored convoys or airplanes.

They've broken the siege and lifted our morale sky high. If they make it back, this letter will be with them. [The jeep track was soon miraculously converted into a passable road capable of carrying loaded trucks. Hacked out of rocky terrain by hand, the rugged trail became known as the "Burma Road," after the supply route built by the Allies during World War II.]

Thank God; finally, a *cease-fire*. It's supposed to last for *thirty days*. This is the first day. To our surprise, it's actually quiet, though I don't have much faith in how long it really will last. But while there's no shelling . . . there is hope.

Last night was just about the limit. The Arabs must have used every Goddamn shell they had before the deadline.

Much love,
*Zippy*

*June 13, 1948*

Dearest Mother, Dad and Naomi,

It is the third day of cease-fire and the quiet is unbearable.

I had a few hours off and came back to my room to catch up on the local news. As luck had it, a guy I was talking to was just about to leave for Tel Aviv — *by plane,* so I'm dashing off a few words for him to mail.

It seems that Israel now has an Air Force and Navy like any normal country. The Jerusalem landing field is right in my backyard. By next week, it should be cleared for regular plane service, if all goes well. Up till now, the airstrip has been a target for incessant shelling: the ground, level one day, is filled with shell holes the next day.

I am still attached to Deir Yassin, now part of the Medical Corps, assigned to two companies. One is the Israeli Army's elite unit, the artillery, what there is of it . . . all three tanks. Don't tell the enemy. There are only two other girls at the base, working in the kitchen, and an assistant who replaces me briefly every forty-eight hours. A woman's paradise.

Our student quarters at Pax have been requisitioned as the area headquarters for the Army. All the officers are my friends so I can always count on mail being delivered to me once it gets to Jerusalem.

I heard the most intriguing rumor — that there is a Jewish Colonel from West Point who is fighting with our forces in the Jerusalem area [Col. David "Mickey" Marcus]. I hope to God it's true.

Have to finish. I'm being rushed by the pilot.

*Zippy*

174

*(Translated from Hebrew)*

Dear Abba,

This letter is being written, literally, at the point of a gun — am being forced to write in Hebrew. Trying my best, but to do that in a rush, at this moment, is no easy task. My comrades-in-arms don't believe I can do it, or that I have a father in America, a Hebrew scholar, who can read it.

What started this off was a call I got a few minutes ago from an American pilot, Jerry Renov, who heard about me through the grapevine and arranged to collect a letter from me before he took off.

My pals, overhearing the conversation, started rushing around looking for writing materials — a pen, paper, an envelope — no simple matter to find here. But, they agreed to do it on one condition only: that I write in Hebrew. Believe me, they are watching like hawks to see that I do.

Sorry I haven't had a chance to write you more about the momentous events that have marked this historic period — we're hardly even conscious of how special they are, probably because we are so completely involved in the events themselves.

We are doing our best to "hold the fort" and hoping we won't have to defend the last ramparts of Jerusalem with our very bodies. It may sound melodramatic, but we have been through one hell of an ordeal and don't have much stamina left for the next round.

You can get used to and learn to live with all kinds of difficulties: being cut off from the world, no mail, no contact with the family, critical shortages of everything, feelings of despair and concern for the future, total and constant fatigue of body and spirit; but what is difficult to take, even impossible to accept, is the loss of friends, people you knew, and even the ones you didn't know. They cannot be forgotten even for a second . . . so many, so terribly many.

Until the present cease-fire was arranged there was hardly a single day or night, barely a single hour without an ever-present barrage of shooting, incessant explosions, merciless shelling, shrieking cries for help, without somebody being killed or wounded. Never a letup from constant fear and terror, never a moment's respite. There was little you could do to protect yourself — cower in a corner, drop to the ground, cover your head with your arms, hold your breath . . . hope that the whining of the missle you heard wasn't meant for you.

How can one describe, summarize, tell the story of this Siege of Jerusalem? The truth of the matter is that it isn't finished yet. When this cease-fire is over, the shooting will no doubt begin again where it left off — only more of it — and we'll respond in kind. More death, more destruction. With no end in sight. Seven Arab states are trying to throttle our vulnerable new State before it has a chance to come into its own. Of these things, it is hard to write.

Just be happy for me that I have been fortunate enough to be here at this time to help give life to this long-yearned-for State. I only hope it gets a chance to grow and thrive in peace.

Your loving daughter,
*Zippy*

Naomi Dear,

I was sitting in the sun daydreaming, thinking what it would be like if, instead of sending this letter, I were to go in person . . .

How I would casually call you up from La Guardia Airport and say, "Hello, Folks. It's me," and listen to your unbelieving squeals. What I would eat in the few short hours before the return trip — steak, salads, coffee, maybe even ice cream? What I would wear: A frilly dress or my sloppy overalls? Shoes with heels or biblical sandals? What would it be like to watch hot and cold water run out of a faucet? How would I feel seeing the familiar skyline of New York, faces, places that I've known all my life? Would there be time for a theater performance? And how would we ever be able to say good-bye again? I sat daydreaming for a long time. I had whole conversations with you and lived real situations — almost.

But, as I'm *not* going anywhere right now, this letter will have to go in my stead and with it my fondest thoughts of you. One thing I know, as sure as I know I'm alive, I couldn't, wouldn't want to stay in America right now. Not for anything.

But I've decided to try and get out of Jerusalem for a short breathing spell. As long as the cease-fire lasts, I can at least try. Chances are slight but I'm determined. I need a change of scenery and circumstances.

I've been interrupted a few times — typical things. A soldier fell off an armored car and hurt his back, the cook snipped off part of a finger and one of the fellows is running a delirious fever for no apparent reason.

Whenever any of these emergencies occur, they yell for "TZIPPY!" clear across the camp. You'd think the telephone hadn't been invented. I get there on the double with my red Magen David knapsack in tow — that's field equipment — and do what I can.

I've discovered that blood is a healthy-looking color and doesn't scare me and I'm intrigued by illnesses that are not run-of-the-mill. I don't know enough medicine to diagnose them but it sure is fun guessing till the doctor arrives and gives them a name. I've only guessed wrong once and that was mistaking mosquito fever for malaria. Well, how was I to know? I've now discovered that there are certain mosquitoes that bring on twenty-four-hour bouts of chills and high fever and then the symptoms disappear as mysteriously as they came.

I see the doc's bicycle in the distance, coming this way. Have to close. My guess about the patient I called him to examine is hepatitis . . . and I hope we don't all catch it.

Love,
*Zippy*

*Jerusalem*

*June 21, 1948*

Dearest Naomi,

This is one letter I may get to mail myself. Am waiting for the next twenty minutes to pass, at which time, if all goes according to schedule, I shall be on my way to Tel Aviv for a few days.

It seemed to me — and everyone else concerned — that after almost two months in Deir Yassin and various other miserable places, I had earned a few days' leave before starting a new assignment. The only trouble is that I had in mind to take my leave out of the city.

So I went straight to the people in charge at Magen David Adom, and flirted and finagled till I got to talk to Mr. Big himself. To him I told the truth: that I had come to Jerusalem directly from America, without ever having seen the country, gone straight into action with never a moment off, intended to stay in Jerusalem but desperately needed to see what the Jewish State looked like. After all, if it hadn't been for people like me, we wouldn't have it.

He looked at me. Picked up his pen. Wrote down something about a wounded boyfriend and passed me orders to "report for duty out of the city today."

I am to accompany a convoy of wounded out of Jerusalem.

Love,
*Zippy*

## *Tel Aviv*

### *June 22, 1948*

Dearest Mother, Dad and Naomi,

It is 6:00 in the morning and I've just awakened from a very bad nightmare in which there was shooting and shelling, hunger and thirst, blood and tension and unbelievable bravery.

I looked around and saw a cozy hotel room with a private bath and someone sleeping in the twin bed.

I listened to the honking of bus horns and neighbors on a nearby balcony arguing. I stared at the ceiling. I'M IN TEL AVIV!

Under the protection of the United Nations a convoy of wounded, which I accompanied for Magen David Adom, was allowed to leave besieged Jerusalem and to pass on the old Jerusalem-Tel Aviv route as far as Latrun — or what remains of it. Before letting us proceed, everybody checked and double-checked us: the Arab Legionnaires checked us, the American representatives checked us, the United Nations representative checked. For what I do not know — we had only bona fide patients with unhealed wounds.

From Latrun we took to the hills, jockeying and rumbling our way to Kfar Bilu, a converted hospital camp, formerly a British Army camp. Most of the patients were amputees and lurching over the rugged terrain was sheer agony for them. How desperately I tried to be cheerful, efficient, to give whatever sympathy and comfort I could.

There, the pain-weary and exhausted patients were given tea and sandwiches with TOMATOES and CUCUMBERS — after months of deprivation. Who could have thought a human being could get so excited about an honest-to-goodness tomato, but all of us did. It tasted of everything I had ever dreamed about eating during hunger pangs in Jerusalem — ice cream, coffee, hamburgers with ketchup, whatever memory or imagination could conjure.

It suddenly dawned on all of us when we arrived that *we were actually in the State of Israel.* A wild and joyous moment, filled with relief and pain and overwhelming excitement. The patients banged their crutches and canes on the ambulance and bus doors. The din was deafening, the exultation uncontrollable.

The boys were sorted into two groups by an Army doctor: those to be kept for treatment and those to be sent for convalescence. I accompanied the convalescent group

180

on to a Tel Aviv rest home. We had started out from Jerusalem at about noon, after much sitting around and waiting for approvals, but it was after 10:30 P.M. when we arrived at the outskirts of Tel Aviv-Jaffa, where the rest home was, and I was able to deliver my patients. Everyone was in high spirits, singing loudly and boisterously, proud of having come from the battlefield of Jerusalem and relieved at being somewhere else.

I started walking the unfamiliar, blacked-out streets, looking for a place to stay. I had brought with me all the money I possessed but that didn't help. Every room in every hotel I tried was either occupied or had been requisitioned by the Army. Finally, bone-tired, hungry, and on the verge of tears, I went to the Military Police, presented my leave pass, told them I had no relatives or friends in town, didn't know my way around, and demanded a bed.

When they heard I had come from Jerusalem, everything moved into high gear; they called a taxi, took me to the proper office, arranged for a bed at the Savoy Hotel and meal tickets at restaurants. One of the fellows even invited me for breakfast, to be followed by a sightseeing tour. I didn't like having to play damsel in distress but it was so good to have somebody worrying about *me* for a change.

At the hotel, I felt so silly getting the thrill I did out of walking up carpeted stairs to a cream-colored room with a tile bathroom — then, turning on the faucet and watching W A T E R stream out. It was so civilized, even the military setup, a far cry from primitive Jerusalem. There we are partisans; here, we are soldiers. My feelings were confirmed a few minutes later when a Palmach girl was brought in to share the room. She had just come from Kiryat Anavim, near Jerusalem, and was feeling very much the same way as I was. Incidentally, she had met up with Carmi and several other of my friends who are fighting in that area. We both rumpled the crisp sheets and tried to relax with a whole cigarette each before going to sleep.

I woke up this morning wondering if all the comforts of Tel Aviv had dissolved during the night; but they were still there, along with glorious sunshine.

I just looked out of the window and discovered that our room overlooks the Mediterranean Sea where people are actually swimming and sunbathing, like Palm Beach or Florida. Incredible.

Strangely, I suddenly longed to be with the boys I had come with. I wished I could have seen their faces, which had been contorted with pain on the difficult journey, suddenly relax into smiles at the sight of plentiful water and food and decent medical equipment.

My first stop this morning will be the Post Office to send you a cable and mail this letter and the twenty other letters that people pushed into my hand as I boarded the convoy. Then I am going to have breakfast with my "date," order a tall glass of orange juice, an egg or two and enough coffee to drown in. Off with the uniform. A casual outfit and saddle shoes. Lady for a day.

Actually three days. *Three whole days and nights* of this paradise.

Love,
*Zippy*

## Tel Aviv

### June 24, 1948

Dearest Mother, Dad and Naomi,

Well, it looks like the war just follows me around. This would have been an ideal vacation except for the bad taste in my mouth over yesterday's "incident." I was sitting with friends at a boardwalk cafe, sipping orangeade, gazing out to sea when, suddenly, the sound of firing was heard from a ship which was not more than two city blocks away from where we were sitting. I am so conditioned to gunfire that I didn't take any particular notice. But everyone else around me froze. This sort of thing doesn't happen in Tel Aviv.

It seems the ship, the *Altalena*, had arrived with hundreds of men and its holds packed with arms and ammunition destined for the Irgun and Stern Gang. Begin, the head of the Irgun, had apparently brought the ship over to ensure reinforcements for *his* people, particularly those in Jerusalem. He hadn't wanted us to agree to the cease-fire in the first place. In effect, he was challenging the authority of the new government and creating an army within an army. Ben-Gurion, who is now Minister of Defense, wasn't about to have that and ordered the ship stopped.

When the shooting started, the Irgun boys who manned the ship jumped overboard and swam ashore; their friends on the beach swam out, under fire, with life buoys to bring in the wounded.

I was shocked. It had come to this? Brother against brother? Jews shooting at Jews?

I somehow cannot see the question from its political or military aspects, all I know is that it was a devastating scene. Now, when every spare moment and resource we have should be used to organize, to train, to prepare for *after* the cease-fire — for it's clear that no agreement for permanent peace will be reached — here we are fighting a civil war.

The firing continued in the streets all day. In the evening there was a siren alert. As it happened, the Army had provided me and a battalion commander from Jerusalem with free tickets to a performance of *Deep are the Roots* at the Ohel Theater and we decided not to miss it.

But, when the siren sounded, the performance was interrupted and everyone went down to the air raid shelter. Nothing like a dark air raid shelter to bring strangers together, especially when they are both Jerusalemites.

After spending three hours in the shelter, we were told that all residents within a mile of the ship had been evacuated from their homes for the night; it was feared that the ship, which was carrying explosives, would blow up and cause terrible damage. As I was billeted at a hotel smack on the seashore, I had no place to go. So my escort and I walked the streets like hundreds of others and finally found a back seat of a car to curl up in.

It was from there that we heard Begin's surrender speech. I hate to admit it, but his voice, high-pitched, hysterical and didactic, sounded every bit like a demagogue. I suppose this kind of treasonable act is intolerable. These extremists should have been stamped out years ago when they were weaker.

It is almost noon now and I am sitting at the same boardwalk cafe close enough to be choked by the smoke from the burning ship, watching the swirling, belching, red-black fire spiral skywards.

I suppose if the *Altalena* were going to explode, it would have done so already.

Love,
*Zippy*

*Tel Aviv*

*June 26, 1948*

Dearest All,

I woke up this morning, sat bolt upright in bed, looked out to the white waves lapping the sea and to the horizon beyond. If the naked eye could see so far, surely a flight of imagination could reach the ends of the earth just as effortlessly — and let you know I am thinking of you. Guess I was feeling sentimental . . . and maybe a little regretful at having to leave the beauty and serenity of the seashore and return to the tension of Jerusalem.

Sitting at a cafe near the hotel for my last Tel Aviv breakfast, I kept seeing familiar faces on the street. It seems like the entire American community has migrated to Tel Aviv. I don't suppose I blame them.

Imagine a waitress asking how many eggs I would like! I've tried very hard not to gorge myself. Most Jerusalemites who return after a leave come back with stomach troubles. It takes a little time to get used to "eating" again.

Had a delightful time last night, dining, dancing, concert — the first performance of the Palestine Philharmonic Orchestra [now the Israel Philharmonic Orchestra] since the establishment of the State. Hearing *Hatikvah* played was a real tearjerker. The Habimah hall is a beautiful theater, Grecian-like columns outside and modern design within. A huge circular building which seats . . . I don't know how many. For a Jerusalemite this is a gigantic place. The largest hall in Jerusalem is a small movie house, probably built in the time of the Turks.

The Palmach seems to be taking over the town today, strutting through the streets as the British used to, wearing battle dress, fingers in fixed position near the trigger, looking grim and warlike. I suppose they are on patrol because the Irgun boys are still on the warpath after the *Altalena* incident; or maybe they are just trying to make an impression. Well, they sure scare me. I'll say one thing for Jerusalem, it may be a dangerous place to live but it has a healthier atmosphere. No artificial war look about it. Women don't primp. The dogs don't look fed and the people in the streets don't look happy — just glad to be alive.

*Later . . .*

I'm marking time waiting for the convoy to be loaded so we can leave for Jerusalem. My bag is stuffed with goodies for my friends back at the base. The regular convoy isn't going out today, so arrangements have been made for me to go by jeep convoy over the Burma Road. I've never ridden in a jeep before.

God, this city is hot. The sweat and dust we are about to kick up on this miracle of road construction is going to make cosmetic history: a new kind of makeup called "Natural Dust," first appearance by yours truly.

This trail we are about to travel is only called a road because by no feat of the imagination does it resemble anything else. Only a few weeks ago it was a donkey trail, the loads hauled over the boulders on the backs of the laborers.

I just got the high sign . . . we're ready to move . . .

Love,
*Zippy*

*Jerusalem*

*June 27, 1948*

Dearest Naomi,

Back in Jerusalem. Another "first": I have just delivered a baby.

Reported to a new assignment this morning, a first aid post in the Sheikh Jarrah area. For the past two months this has been the front, and probably, the minute hostilities are resumed, will be again. The building is bullet-ridden and pockmarked with shell holes. Formerly, it was a Hadassah prenatal and infant-care station but during the cease-fire some of the old clients in the neighborhood are using the facilities.

Spent the early hours arranging the station, listing things I would need, scrubbing up and getting acquainted with the surroundings. Suddenly, there were screams from the porch and a pregnant woman was dragged in, howling in French that she had "dropped the baby."

Thank God for the neighbor who brought her in. Together, we did the job in twenty minutes flat; with nature doing most of the work. A makeshift setup — a hard slab of table — but adequate. Speaking half French/half Hebrew, I learned that the mother had eight children, and a husband fighting in the Galilee. She was so grateful it hadn't happened in a shelter during a shelling raid. Too many people, she said.

As I ran for blanket, towels and other things, and as I held her head and gripped her arms to help still the pain, I found myself thinking a horrible thought: what cruelty to bring a child into this hateful world.

The baby gave a lusty cry. I looked at him for the first time. What a revelation birth is. A miracle of humanity. As I bundled them off to the hospital, I couldn't help thinking . . . another boy, another soldier!

This is a very poor, underprivileged neighborhood — a real slum area. Dirty. Neglected. An eyesore. There is no sense removing the sandbags and stones that are stacked in the window frames, even though they shut out light and air. The cease-fire is too fragile. I try not to think about it.

But I can't help thinking that here we are with no electricity, no water, the food situation only slightly eased; and only two hours away from the peaceful Paradise I have just left — Tel Aviv — with its *everything* in abundance. True, everybody there worries about Jerusalem but Tel Aviv barely feels the war or shows any scars.

I finally received some back mail, from early April, stamped *Czechoslovakia Airport*—FIRST FLIGHT TO ISRAEL. It was heartwarming to think that it had traveled in a mail sack snuggled up with a cargo of arms and ammunition which our pilots have been ferrying to Israel since the war started.

Rushing to finish . . .

Love,
*Zippy*

---

*Jerusalem*

*July 3, 1948*

Dearest Everybody,

I've been transferred to a new base, Permanent Camp No. 2 in Talpiot. Camp nurse, in charge of the infirmary and the infirm. At first glance, everybody looked decidedly healthy: big strapping guards and lean, wiry officers.

The guards escorted me to the *mateh* (HQ), passing through a labyrinth of corridors and closed doors to the door of the Commander. The desk seemed much too big for him until he spoke and then the room seemed much too small for his voice, which echoed in a boom to the walls and back. He read my credentials carefully, asked me where I had been before and then took me on a cook's tour of the layout.

Since this camp was formerly a British Army barracks, there are very classy officers' quarters — dining room and recreation hall, richly decorated with furnishings confiscated from the neighboring Arab houses.

What a stuffy setup though. We eat separately from the "ranks" — same grub, just dressed up and served up more slowly with supposedly more atmosphere. Instead of coffee being poured at you while you hold the cup, it is presented to you cold, already in the cup, by a shadowy hand from the left side who places it precisely at right angles to your nose. After coffee, you rise ceremoniously and deposit yourself gracefully with lighted cigarette in one of the luxurious chairs. You sit till your cigarette is finished and then back to work, as if you were full and satisfied. I can tell you all this slow motion stuff doesn't dull my appetite a bit.

As this is a "permanent camp," I am, more or less, permanently attached to it, until someone on a whim sends me elsewhere. I'm not so sure I can stomach this strictly military atmosphere for long. One thing we seemed to have learned from His Majesty's Armed Forces is "officership." Officers are officers, the ranks are the ranks and never the twain shall mix. Maybe it's just in this place.

There are some 250 men and me, the only "lady" in the camp at the moment. They wanted to pamper me so I was taken by the Sergeant Major and three hefty men on a tour of Arab houses to choose furniture suitable for my four-walled cell. I guess my experience in Deir Yassin cured me of pangs of remorse about appropriating private property for camp use. I found beds, night tables, mirrors, a glass-topped desk, curtains and knickknacks to make the infirmary efficient, cozy and comfy.

I think I was sent here because I seem to have acquired a reputation in the Medical Corps for being good at improvising and organizing first aid stations.

Daddy will be very proud to learn that my Hebrew is so good that I spent a whole day here before anyone discovered I was an American and that only happened because the visiting doctor in charge is German-speaking and doesn't know Hebrew well. We found the best common language to be English, which he does know well, having been in the British Army for a long time.

The other day, we were officially sworn into the Israeli Army, along with all the soldiers of Israel at camps and bases throughout the country. An Oath of Allegiance; an impressive parade. From underground partisans in the Haganah, we have now become soldiers of the Israel Defense Forces, the first Jewish Army in two thousand years. What a proud moment! We danced, sang, drank and cried. Also held a solemn ceremony in memory of those who had fallen.

I refuse to speculate about the political situation. There are only a few more days to go before the cease-fire is scheduled to end and then . . . who knows?

Love,
*Zippy*


*Jerusalem*

*July 13, 1948*

Dearest Mother and Dad,

I'm in luck. My friend Yehudah popped in to visit me at camp and will take this letter for mailing in Tel Aviv. He was in both the Ramleh and Lydda battles and says we are stronger than ever before — wiped out the Arab Legion strongholds in forty-eight hours. I only hope we don't sign a truce *now*. It would be a shame if we had to stop just when we could actually *win* the war by ourselves; well, not really by ourselves. Only if we continue to get supplies and help "unofficially."

The fifty dollars you sent me a couple of months ago, also a package with some wonderful things, finally reached me. I've distributed most of the edibles among my housekeeping friends. After all, in the Army I get three meals a day. As for the money, I'm delighted to have it. Pay in the Army is only two pounds a month and even that we haven't seen.

It's funny, though, there really isn't a thing you can do with money. There is nothing to be purchased and no time to go make purchases. A day off consists of going to the house of somebody who has water, taking a sponge bath out of a small tin and eating different combinations of the same crap you get at camp. I shouldn't complain. The food situation is better than the nil it was.

All the Americans kids are fine, and you can report that to their families. Most of my close friends are in Tel Aviv, attached to Air Force Headquarters, and they are trying to get me transferred there as well. We'll see.

Love,
*Zippy*

*P.S.*

Incidentally, the rumor that there was an American West Pointer fighting with us was true but, unfortunately, he was accidentally killed the night before the cease-fire ended. His name was David "Mickey" Marcus. Our camp has been named in his honor, Camp Stone — "Stone" was his alias in Israel.

*With the cease-fire ended and no possibility to send mail out of the country from beleaguered Jerusalem, I began making entries in a notebook in diary form. The entries — the "letters" that follow — were eventually torn from the notebook and sent off a month later.*

*Jerusalem*

*July 14, 1948*

Dear Me,

The Arabs refused Bernadotte's mediation efforts for a thirty-day extension of the cease-fire. WE'RE BACK TO WAR AGAIN!

Last night was a misery. From our backyard in the outskirts of the city, heavy artillery was relentlessly being directed at Arab strongholds toward the south. Explosion after explosion, each blast thundering through my ears, jolting my sleepy thoughts. The mosquitoes were unbearable. As I am writing this more to myself than to you, I can bare my soul. I had nightmares like I have never had before. I wanted to reach out and hold onto them but the thunder of the guns chased them away, only not before shattering them into mosquito rain that sprayed and attacked my body with a hail of shrapnel.

I woke in a sweat, fearful of lighting the kerosene lamp lest it disclose our position. In the moonlight, I mixed up a paste of bicarbonate of soda and water and covered my arms and face with it to ease the gnawing, burning, itching. Then I crawled back to bed, listening till the thunder lulled me to sleep . . . and another nightmare. Bloody bodies hurling through space. I saw them vividly, clearly, till the dawn blurred the picture and silenced the guns.

Breakfast this morning was also a nightmare — cold tasteless food and irritating conversation. The make-believe coffee tasted worse than ever and I reached for a cigarette. Maybe it was the rustle of the wrapping paper or a natural development but, suddenly, they were all aware of me. They wanted my opinion about Americans fighting in the war. I couldn't help thinking of Mickey Marcus and didn't feel like sharing my thoughts with them, so I made a feeble excuse to escape from the room.

At moments like this, I miss the nice young doctor who had been assigned to us for a while and helped fill the heavy hours. Talking to him was always good. The arrangement was great until he got promoted to Regimental Physician to replace someone who was killed.

Scrubbed the floors with Lysol, dusted around and then chatted with the patients who came in for pills, fresh bandages or just a "shmoose." One of the boys, who had been with *Etzel* and still considers his soul to be with them, proceeded to brainwash me with the ideological aims, principles and methods of operation of the organization. He told me his side of the tale of terrorism. Why, for example, the King David Hotel had to be blown up; he had been in on it. I just clamped up. I have stopped trying to argue with anyone. On the job, I receive patients calmly, smilingly, warmly, and wonder how I do it; because inside I am all churned up, upset, unnerved and wrung-out as I have never been before.

*Next day . . .*

Last night there was an air raid. I dreamt about you, Naomi. You always liked plane trips. You were sitting beside the pilot, flirting with him while he dropped bombs that exploded not far away from me. I didn't get out of bed — I felt safe because I knew you would dissuade him from hurting me or those around me . . . I am still here this morning.

*July 16, 1948*

While rummaging among the vandalized Arab houses in the neighborhood searching for furnishings for my infirmary, I found some books. One, in particular, caught my eye, *Short Stories of Thomas Hardy.* I borrowed the book and read a few of the stories, not in the order presented, just picked at random, trying to associate a title with a particular mood. But all of them left me pondering the irony of fate; a familiar theme of Hardy. It was an eerie reminder of our insignificance: we are no more than insects on earth, escaping death by a mere whim of some unseen fate-maker.

My pensive mood was broken by a knock at the door, a dripping of blood, followed by a quivering body — Eli. I attended to his wound quickly and efficiently, marveling at my calmness and warmth. Although I don't like him as a person, I felt eased by his gratefulness, his relief.

He chatted with me; it seemed to make him feel better. He says the word is out that another truce is to be announced for tomorrow. That means tonight will be FIRE AND HELL. A truce period with no permanent solution in sight. It's ridiculous, useless.

*       *       *

An army that lights candles and blesses them on Friday night. Over the soup plates and the flowers on the table and the shiny faces of our khaki-clad soldiers, I saw the candles blinking at me and my eyes brimmed with tears. For a moment, I was with you, wrapped in the warmth of our family Friday nights — and then I was back listening to the news . . .

*   *   *

The Sergeant Major just came in to tell me we are on Full Alert — this is the final hour before the enforced truce, accepted this afternoon, goes into effect. Every last drop of energy will be used by us and the Arabs to push forward as far as possible. Already the bombardment is deafening.

Aharon, the Welfare Officer, just called his wife. *"Elohim yishmereinu,"* he said. God preserve and watch over us. How much we need such a blessing tonight . . .

*July 17, 1948*

God, last night was awful, but not as awful for us as for those up front. The shells fell close. The house shook, the air was charged with explosives, one following the other relentlessly. No one knew a moment of peace until 5:30 A.M., when suddenly — synchronized silence.

I must have dozed off then for a bit. A nightmare about swimming in an ocean of blood and not being able to open my eyes underwater.

I woke up drenched in sweat, devoured by mosquito bites, with deep circles under my eyes, and listened hard for the sound of the trucks and buses bringing back our boys from the forward positions.

Heard that Nazareth was taken. The Old City Wall penetrated. Two friends seriously wounded. I've got a pass to get to the hospital . . .

*July 18, 1948*

The first day of cease-fire was a farce. I almost got myself killed three times today by mortar shells which fell indiscriminately in town. I was determined to get to Pax to pick up mail and messages and thumbed a ride with an *Etzelnik* on a motorcycle.

It almost seemed as if we were being followed. We barely passed a spot when BANG the spot was gone with a cloud of flying stones — and so it went. There was no stopping at that point — open spaces, not a building in sight. We put on the gas, steadied our helmets and raced for the main street and a shelter. Well, I got my mail and it was worth it. I kept thinking how silly that scene was. Me and a terrorist on flying wheels. What a title for a film!

*July 20, 1948*

Am sitting vigil while the Regimental Doctor and the Chief Medical Orderly sleep. They came to visit — more social than anything else — saw beds that had been sprayed with DDT and couldn't resist. They hadn't slept for days.

Our steel helmets with the bold imprint of Magen David Adom are lined up on the floor looking like bowling balls with a company trade mark. A barricade blocking the exit.

*July 29, 1948*

Looks like the cease-fire truce is really here to stay for a while . . .

I've been busy relaxing. Am using my off-time to attend soldiers' concerts, dances, visit bedridden friends, sunbathe and generally not exert myself. And believe me, writing is exerting. It takes a special kind of energy to sit down and try to find words to express the multitude of complex emotions, thoughts, impressions that invade me in the course of a day. Summed up, they might be called "GRIMMS — Very GRIM Fairy Tales."

Now that I have a few free undisturbed hours, I find my mind is lazy. My thoughts have dried up. I am drained, my imagination throttled. Numb . . .

## Part Seven

# The War Stands Still

*August 1, 1948*

Dearest Naomi,

It's my birthday. By way of a present, I received word this morning that I have been officially transferred to Air Force HQ in Tel Aviv and in the next few days will probably be sent off to the BIG CITY. In a way, I indirectly asked for this release from nursing responsibilities. Now that the truce looks stable for a while, my friends in Tel Aviv are encouraging me to get back to some normalcy and try to work in my own field. Aside from that news, it's not much of a birthday — though, in this country, just to be alive and healthy at *any* age is an achievement. So I should count my blessings.

I wish to hell this war was over . . . It's gumming up so many things, among them my personal life. The threshold is cluttered with suitors — all of them eligible, wonderful, intelligent men whom I genuinely like. But for the present, at least, I have put up a friendly "Do Not Disturb" sign. I know I am just jabbering, dashing off words to fill up a page I foolishly started. And, having started, there's no stopping.

This letter is Tel Aviv-bound to be mailed, together with a pile of scribblings I've been writing in diàry form, to give you some idea of what's been going on . . .

Love,
*Zippy*

Dearest All of You,

As you can see from the address, I am in Tel Aviv. Billeted at the Excelsior Hotel on Hayarkon Street not far from Air Force Headquarters and half a block from the beach.

What the hell will I be doing here? That's a question I am still trying to figure out. I only arrived a day or two ago and am busy meeting interesting people and being offered the choicest of jobs. The Israeli Air Force is just "getting off the ground"; there are some intriguing work possibilities. But since most of my American friends, including Nat Cohen and Carmi, are set up in Intelligence/Public Relations work, that's probably where I'll end up. Please don't discuss this with anyone.

After all we went through in Jerusalem, I feel a new zest for life. Life in this city means clothes. Tel Aviv women dress with such flair, I feel like a provincial; you'd never think I was born and brought up in New York. Probably soon there will be an official notice requiring us to be in uniform all the time, which I won't mind. Looks good on me. But right now I need some clothes for after hours. In Air Force HQ, we work strictly office hours; when you are through for the day, you're a civilian unless there is something special cooking and you are on duty. It's like normal living again, almost.

One of the pilots on this floor is leaving for the States early in the morning and offered to take a letter and bring regards. He is one of the overseas volunteers — veteran transport pilots, fighter pilots and pilots of light planes — without whom we wouldn't be able to carry on this war. I met him this afternoon. I had just come back from swimming with my hair drenching wet and remembered I had a date. In the late afternoon, all the sunshine is on the other side of the building, so, in order to dry my hair, I sneaked out onto the boys' balcony and caught them in their BVDs. Now that we are "intimately" acquainted, I'll let this guy treat me to a three-cent stamp and a five-cent phone call. I hope he remembers to call.

It's a shame about these volunteer pilots going back. I can't find the words or arguments to dissuade them. Actually, they came here mentally and emotionally unprepared for what they found. Perhaps, if they had been exposed to real life situations — a little of Jerusalem — and not just to activity up in the air, the pettiness of their complaints would be more realistic.

What they seem to forget is that the Israeli Army is only a couple of months old and the Air Force less than that, so how can it be expected to stand up in comparison with the American or British Air Force traditions, which took hundreds of years to develop? I suppose nobody is really interested in stopping their return. They are not Zionists, they are not idealists, most of them are not even Jews; adventurists who simply came to do a job, for which I hear some of them are getting paid.

Am beginning to unwind — swimming, dancing, dinner, lunch and breakfast dates. A concert tonight. Visited the zoo, the park. Enjoying — till I start work.

Much love,
*Zippy*

*P.S.*

Here's one for a laugh: I read in the papers that the British are agonizing over how to announce an agreement they made with Israel to restore postal services — suspended on May 15th — when they have refused to recognize the State. To help them out of the dilemma, it was suggested to the British Foreign Office that instead of mentioning "Israel" they announce that postal services are being restored between Britain and 230 post offices — and then list all 230 post offices. Apparently, they are still puzzling over it.

## Tel Aviv
### August 10, 1948

Naomi Dear,

The concert the other night gave me a jolt. It made me realize that, though I appear to be fully relaxed, I'm still not entirely over Jerusalem "battle fatigue." I was invited to the concert by Yehudah. When everyone else found it difficult to get tickets, he managed to obtain two. Having been triumphant thus far, he was elated and eager for the performance to begin. I, for some reason, was very passive.

The hall was full with too many people, sitting, waiting, sweating, fanning the summer heat into each other's faces. Yehudah pointed knowingly at the majestic crop of white hair two rows in front of us — a great painter (Reuven Rubin); at the lady in black with a half smile on her face — our first Minister to Russia (Golda [Meir] Myerson); at the grey suit and the black moustache — our first Foreign Minister (Moshe [Sharett] Shertok); and when our Prime Minister, B-G (David Ben-Gurion) entered, everyone clapped in recognition.

The conductor (Izler Solomon) decided it was time to put in an appearance, and the concert was on. The Prime Minister opened his tie and the first two buttons of his shirt. The Foreign Minister removed his grey jacket. The lady with the half smile looked pensive. The white crop two rows ahead whispered something to a black arrangement who bent her coiffure forward to see what had been pointed out and revealed a lovely suntanned neck choked by a double string of pearls and black velvet. The neck extended down and down until it met up with a grey print material somewhere below my line of vision.

By the time I had settled down ready to be carried away by the music, the first number was over and people were applauding. We didn't have a program but something in the earnest look on the musicians' faces led me to believe that the next piece was to be a serious one. The conductor raised his arms dramatically — he didn't have a baton. Suddenly, the arms were followed by his shoulders, his head, his whole body . . . swaying, flowing in fascinating movements, with the grace of a ballet dancer.

It was then that I began to lose touch with the heat, the faces, the white-shirted musicians and the "ballet dancer." I was carried out to sea, in a flimsy boat, to a mad ocean with furious waves. The sea calmed, the boat landed and I was in a new country. So this was the Holy Land and this its Holy City. I heard the thud, the passing whizz, the whistling, whining sounds, and then everything exploded. The music had stopped abruptly. I raised my head and saw a body floating in blood, a little child with deep black shiny eyes; I found myself staring at a woman in a red dress with shiny black buttons.

The Prime Minister mopped his forehead and the sides of his face with a ball of white handkerchief. The lady in black leaned back contentedly. The conductor's arms were spread out like the wings of an airplane and the music soared again. It banged against the windows and the pillars, it shattered the ceiling, collapsed and fell into a heap of rubble and flying plaster . . . one great big heap of crushed stone and people in the middle of Jerusalem's Ben-Yehudah Street . . .

*Tel Aviv*

*August 14, 1948*

Dearest All of You,

My neighbors on Hayarkon Street include the *first ever* Ambassadors to Israel from both America and Russia. Our man, James McDonald, got a very enthusiastic reception on his arrival the day before yesterday — I was there. He is a very welcome figure here, mostly because of his own personality and the fact that he is known to be a friend of Israel.

I happened to be passing by the Gat Rimon Hotel just as he was expected to arrive, so I hopped onto a nearby balcony and had a first-rate view of the entire proceedings. I may even be in the newsreel. One of my Pathé News friends kept his camera pinned right on me most of the time.

Our Military Police, decked out handsomely in fancy uniforms, escorted the cavalcade of cars and jeeps to the hotel door. The Ambassador's party emerged from their cars to clapping and warm cheers from the crowd. The Soldiers' Club also happens to be nearby, so there was no shortage of people to greet him. He reappeared outside several times to smile at the crowd and face the photographers. At that point, I took my fifty paces to my own digs for a cold shower and a change of clothing.

The funniest and most ironic note about the welcome was that, atop the hotel, the American flag was flying to the right, the Russian flag to the left and, gently floating in the hot breeze in the center, the Israeli blue and white. I couldn't help chuckling at the thought that we had managed to bring together on one roof these two great powers, at odds on so many other fronts, with us in the middle.

As part of my new job I'm supposed to get to know places and facts, so the other day I made a tour of outposts in the Haifa area — airfields, new camp site, radar station, training school — keeping track of things that are happening for those who will someday write the history of the Air Force. Staff car and driver. Very classy. Have a sinking feeling that I'll hate myself for getting into this outfit — it's not my kind of thing.

Love,
*Zippy*

*Tel Aviv*

*August 18, 1948*

Hello,

It's impossible to concentrate with the noisy goings-on around me: the pilots in the next room arguing over a poker game, music blaring at a cafe close by, a hilarious party down the hall. I can't even hear my fingers pattering over the keys. So, between the oppressive heat, the riot around me and my non-writing mood, all energy has been squelched and memory wiped out.

Did I tell you that the author Arthur Koestler, who is here as a war correspondent, has a room at a hotel right across the street and his balcony faces ours? It was he — unbeknown to him — who inspired me to sit down and force myself to write this letter. I came back to my room, hot and tired and all ready to throw myself into bed when, suddenly, I happened to glance across the street and saw Koestler plodding away at his typewriter. "Well," said I to myself, "if he can produce under these conditions, I can at least try."

Incidentally, this damn Army is is so poor it can't even allocate typewriters: I lug my portable back and forth to the office every day, mainly for my own convenience.

This morning, instead of checking the typewriter as he should have, the guard at the entrance to the building was busy looking at me. Pinned to my shirt — left of second button going down — is the Israel Air Force insignia, a little silver airplane. He fingered it playfully and said — it sounds better in Hebrew — "I not only like the airplane, I even like the airfield." As I can't get to my desk without going past this guy, you can imagine the mood I was in even before starting the day. Tel Avivians have no subtlety.

Stopped for lunch at a Tnuvah dairy. Clean and cheap, typical local food: chopped eggplant salad, a tomato and a cold drink. Followed by three cigarettes.

On the way home, feeling kind of blue — I'm not attuned to Tel Aviv yet — I treated myself to some flowers I couldn't resist, lovely red and white carnations with a deep cinnamon smell that penetrates right to your nostrils. I had hardly finished putting them in water when my roommate, the Head Nurse in the Air Force, arrived and announced that it was her birthday. So, the flowers came in handy after all.

It's no use. I'm abandoning the effort and joining the merrymakers, though I'm not sure what the hilarity is about. Might as well contribute my share. I see Koestler has also stopped.

Love,
*Zippy*

Please confine yourself to V-mail forms or lightweight letters. We seem to have adopted the irritating British tradition of checking thick or suspicious-looking mail for explosives, contraband or money. For me, it means a time-consuming and annoying trip to the Post Office.

*Tel Aviv*

*September 2, 1948*

Naomi Dear,

Went to a performance of the Hebrew Opera the other night with John Roy Carlson (author of the book *Undercover*) and had a perfectly wonderful time.

I keep bumping into the big shot American Zionists who are here for a conference; their hotel is just down the street. We smile, stop to chat, they tell me how well I look and prod me with inane questions like, "Are you going to stay, my dear?"

"Well, yes, I like this country. Why don't you try it for a while?"

And a guy like S. answers, "I can't see it myself. As you know, I am against *chalutziut*. Primitive country this. Has no future."

What the hell is a guy like that doing representing Zionists?

Or Mr. F. who whispered in my ear that he is about to take a "secret" flying trip to the Negev and Jerusalem — a trip he couldn't possibly take without Air Force Intelligence knowing about it — which means me. When he returned, he offered the profound observation that "things are not as dangerous as they were cracked up to be."

"Jerusalem is quiet," says he, familiarly pinching my cheek, "and all the time we thought you were starved and deprived. You look fine."

Well, I don't feel so Goddamn fine, I'd like to tell him. Especially when I see him and his cronies parked at the most expensive hotels in Tel Aviv, squandering the hard-earned pennies that some of us used to knock ourselves out collecting for the cause. Lest we forget — the Zionist cause. Now, the "leaders" have appeared in droves to lay claim to THEIR property, give a quick look around and pronounce themselves experts on the state of the new State.

On the other hand, there is our mutual friend Z. who doesn't say anything outright but implies in every sentence the futility of her life in America as compared to the alive feeling she gets in *Aretz* (the Land). But then there is her personal inability to see herself at her age in such surroundings, "divorced from the frustrations of America and having to face the frustrations here." Kibbutz doesn't appeal to her. She dreads going back to her groove, yet cannot find it in herself to think in terms of settling here.

Though I was tempted to tell her that every person here counts, I couldn't, because in her case, all reason is against it. We could spare her. Wars are only glamorous from the distance, especially righteous wars fought for survival, a better way of life or an ideal. Living in a country at war, even if the war is temporarily in a truce, can cut additional precious years out of one's personal life. To be avoided if possible. This is truly a very difficult country to live in. Somehow, I cannot see her with her love of luxury adjusting to what she will find here. It is too far a cry from America.

I also told her it would be better to come married, for practical reasons. Most of the best element get married very young here — 18, 19, 20 — both men and women. I don't think it's easy to marry a man who hasn't the slightest understanding of your background. It may be fun, novel and interesting to go out with such a man but to marry? You'd want someone with whom you have something in common — outlook, background, a set of standards. Not just a man who is attracted to you, admires your personality, your brand of Zionism and, perhaps most of all, your American passport.

Actually, I spent a whole evening dissuading her, sounding pessimistic and terribly down to earth. On the other hand, one of the most frustrating things I myself could possibly imagine at this moment would be to return to America, back to Zionist meetings and District politics, back to TALKING, TALKING AND JUST TALKING. Here life is an exciting and constant challenge and I thrive on it.

Am leaving day after tomorrow for a three-day trip to the Galilee with a group of Americans, Canadians, South Africans, British, etc. — "Anglo-Saxons" — organized by the Air Force to give us a chance to see the country. Anything to get out of this city.

Love,
*Zippy*

## Tel Aviv

### September 17, 1948

Dear Everybody,

The assassination of Bernadotte probably left you all in shock. The same here. It is hard to accept cold-blooded murder! Strategically and politically it was a tragedy; also a slap in the face for us. Must be the Stern Gang at it again.

My work now is excruciatingly routine and strictly behind the desk, accomplished by sitting on one's "whatsis" till distraction. That, and making dots, dots and more dots on complicated maps till I find myself dreaming of coordinates colliding in the same grid and erupting into a global confrontation. The pace is not as yet maddening because the war is at a standstill. I'm certainly not overworked; but I sure am bored, with only myself to blame.

Actually, the work is important — I shouldn't minimize it. It's also pleasant and companionable. I am working with Nat and Carmi and a score of other good friends and some new ones who are very nice. But it is like fighting the war from the Pentagon building. You know before anyone else does what is going on all the time, and yet you aren't really participating at all — not in the true meaning of the word and certainly not with any creative personal contribution.

I have a new roommate, from Sweden, a product of the ghetto, concentration camps, and parents killed before her eyes — all in a matter of ten years. A girl of twenty who has roamed the world for half of her life and yet is unspoiled and undaunted in spirit. She has been in the country even less time than I and already jabbers away in Hebrew picked up during a year in a Cyprus detention camp.

We went to a movie last night accompanied by some of the Russian boys from the tank unit who were stationed with me in Jerusalem and are here on leave. I was flabbergasted to hear her prattle with one in Hebrew, another in Polish and Russian and a third in Hungarian. The movie was in English, with us heckling in Yiddish.

It is like meeting the world sitting in one place. Of all the international types I have met here, I think the South Africans are the nicest lot. One by one, they are gems — most of them products of the Habonim Zionist youth movement. The proportion of Zionists among them is larger than in any other national representation — people who know what they came for — excluding the Canadians, who are my second choice for nice guys.

Of course, I should be working at this very moment. Everyone, no doubt, thinks that I am; I have on a diligent and preoccupied look.

Anyhow, the war simply cannot start until I finish my map . . . but it'll have to wait until I finish this letter.

Love,
*Zippy*

*Tel Aviv*

*October 2, 1948*

Naomi Dear,

The radio broadcast a special Rosh Hashanah message from Leonard Bernstein who came to conduct the Palestine Philharmonic. He was wonderfully moving, spoke straight from the heart, including a few words in Hebrew.

Somehow, Rosh Hashanah and holidays in general were meant for families to celebrate, not individuals. I've been invited to several families for meals, but it's not the same thing. And right afterwards to rush back to work. It's incongruous: from synagogue to war room. But that's the way it is.

I hope this will truly be one of the happiest years ever. As far as I'm concerned, one way of fulfilling that wish would be to have one or all of you here. I'm counting on that, and soon.

Naomi, I know how you feel and appreciate your conflict — to come or not to come. What I am about to say may sound empty of idealism; rather, it is based on experience. For me, the only way to deal with a conflict of this sort or to extricate myself from a groove I'd rather not be in is to *plunge*. No purpose is served by agonizing over the decision. DO something — *anything*, but make it ACTION. Either pick yourself up and go to California, if that's what is attracting you, or pick up and come here. If you are thinking of coming at all, *come*. The excuse about no job, no money, no man, is just so much stalling. All you need is carfare and a little push. Don't look back — look ahead.

As for me, the "vacation" feeling in Tel Aviv is over. I am beginning to get restless, with a yen to get back to the real work of the war. The atmosphere in Tel Aviv reminds me too much of New York without any of its advantages — competitive, superficial and in no way uplifting.

The lifestyle here is also draining me financially: the token food allowance — 600 mils a day (about two dollars) — and the token Air Force salary don't go very far. A roll of film, a bottle of eau de cologne, or a dress to the cleaners can upset your entire monthly budget, which was operating on a deficit to begin with. The other day, I felt my stomach ought to be treated to a little boiled chicken and, rather than lose my appetite at the outset, didn't ask the price. Even with my 10 percent service discount, I paid 840 mils for just a main dish, with nothing but a small salad.

Of course, I could have gone to the new Soldiers' Canteen and been given a sandwich — mostly thick bread — and some horrible ersatz coffee for only a couple of mils, but with that would come noise, waiting in line, the heat and being kibbitzed. No way to relax and enjoy the food. Lunch and dinner dates are plentiful but, generally, we all go "Dutch treat" because most of us are in the same predicament.

A very happy and healthy New Year to you.

Love,
*Zippy*

*Tel Aviv*

*October 10, 1948*

Dear All,

As of this morning I was transferred back to the Medical Corps — but this time to the Air Force Medical Corps. Was supposed to have left for the environs of Haifa today, but the doctor assigned to go with me is sick so we've been detained for a couple of days.

I'll be the NCO in charge of the infirmary and sick bay that we'll be setting up for all Air Force personnel in the Haifa area. In addition to the doctor and myself, there'll be three medical orderlies and an ambulance driver. We'll be stationed in a former British Army building compound, now being used as training base for Air Force ground and maintenance crews. It is basically a school environment. Probably not half as interesting as the two other choices I had at airfields, but I'll be doing work I like, with the responsibility I need.

I think I am doing the right thing by leaving Tel Aviv. Hayarkon Street is *not* Israel; to keep a healthy perspective, I need a little distance from it.

I've been on a real merry-go-round since I came to Tel Aviv. Out practically every night for two months with all kinds and types of people. It's been fun, sort of, but enough

215

is enough. I truly regret the day I left Jerusalem — perhaps getting back to nursing will set things straight again.

In any case, the Air Force is getting organized; the department I am now with will be moving to Jaffa shortly and that really will be an intolerable situation — female soldiers in an IAF camp, women's barracks, officers' mess, spit and polish, saluting and rank-pulling — the whole bit. The war may be standing still but bureaucracy in the military is moving ahead at a fast pace.

In Haifa, I'll be boss in my own setup where, for one thing, more Hebrew is spoken. Air Force HQ is practically English-speaking — most of the personnel and pilots are Anglo-Saxons, trained in the British, Canadian, American and South African Air Forces.

Incidentally, Carmi never had and hasn't got malaria. How do these stupid stories originate? About three months ago, he had yellow jaundice but that was after Jerusalem and much undernourishment. It is surprising more of us didn't have worse aftereffects than we did. As for me, I haven't had anything worse than a common cold since I've been here.

During the siege of Jerusalem I did break out in something the doctor thought was the beginning of pellagra but some vitamin B tablets fixed me up in no time. Really, it's amazing what a good health record I've had this past year. Perhaps treating sick people and seeing what stupid illnesses they incur carelessly makes you expend the extra energy to take care of yourself. So many people here suffer from stomach ulcers, boils and dysentery — often just from carelessness in diet and hygiene. So, knowing how simple it is to avoid these things, I steer clear.

Have to run . . .

Dearest Family,

Perhaps it's me or the year that has passed since the last time I was at Ginegar, but something has changed. This time, I felt at home at the kibbutz. I have lost the self-consciousness of an outsider, the awareness of me and what I am wearing, or saying or doing. I'm at home not only in Ginegar but in all of Israel. It's my country, I own the place — I'm fighting for it.

I speak the language — its main vocabulary is *chutzpah*, initiative, banging on the table when you want something and, though griping louder than the next one, accepting and resigning yourself to a greater degree than you ordinarily would — out of understanding, love.

Left the kibbutz early to find a ride to Haifa to catch a bus to the base. No traffic. Nothing came along, so I started to walk. The sun was hot and my pack was heavy. I looked out over the *Emek*, stretching for miles around with its green patches and misty hills in the background and felt I was walking on air — me, the silence of the *Emek* and not a living thing in sight.

The magic was broken when a jeep pulled up and three fellow soldiers hauled me in, with a cowboy yelp that would have woken Rip Van Winkle. I must have been in a trance. It seems I walked over three miles and hadn't even realized it.

Love,
*Zippy*

*October 29, 1948*

Mother Dear,

Believe me, the doomsday report you got is way off the mark. Probably from one of those people who hop over to Israel briefly, stick their heads through two doors, have a gossipy luncheon and go home loaded with "inside information." They know as much about what makes the wheels go round here as the average American does about what cooks in Washington, D.C. The nonsense these gossip-hungry people gobble up is often tasteless leftovers someone dished out mindlessly.

Take it for a fact that I am more familiar with the scene after a year here than your "here today gone tomorrow" observer who saw only a negative picture in stark black and white. What he failed to fathom was what lies below the surface and motivates most of the people who live here: fierce dedication and uncompromising faith, an unbeatable combination. Israel's capability cannot be measured by any standard yardstick. It defies reason. It has to do with self-sacrifice, resourcefulness and steadfast determination. An outsider can't really assess it. You have to see these people in action to understand what makes this country tick. They're incredible.

One learns a lot about tolerance here. It takes a lot of it to live with your fellow Jews. But I can't help getting damn angry, and protective, when something I value and hold dear is maligned, degraded and diminished. We here can't afford to dwell on our faults and shortcomings, and resent it when someone else points them out — as if we didn't know about them.

Looked at from the outside in, one could easily label this country a disaster, a land of primitive people, living in backward and isolated ignorance. And that is partially true. But, at the same time, there are dynamic forces at work and an ever-increasing number of people fighting for change — even if they are fogged by idealism, blind nationalism and overconfidence fed on partisanship.

There aren't words broad enough to begin to generalize about the heterogeneity of this country — its people, cities, settlements and kibbutzim. Israel is a melting pot like America never was. A tiny sponge of a land, which in the short span of a year has had to absorb into its fighting forces soldiers, who aren't soldiers at all, from every continent in the world. Their only baggage: culture, customs and tongues from foreign lands. They and their baggage were dumped here, for lack of any other address, in the midst of a bloody war, and no one has had time to open this Pandora's box and sort it out.

Such a little, pathetic, struggling State to have such a multitude of internal problems, so many of them seemingly insurmountable. Not to mention the ever-present horde of Arab states pressing menacingly at our borders in an unfinished war. It takes a lot of tolerance, compassion and understanding to accept all the things that are wrong, and a lot of courage and physical stamina to stand your ground regarding things that could or should be changed.

In the Army, it's the insignificant things that make a difference, become all-consuming: wanting a winter uniform when you are cold or a leave pass when you need to get away, stomaching inexperienced officers and ridiculous military discipline, seeing people stepping over other people in a hurry to get ahead, watching all the vanities of life at work, the spoils system at its worst . . .

In about ten years' time this will be a great country. Now, it is chaos; still in the throes of birth pains while the miracle emerges — with plenty of bloodshed.

I didn't mean to get carried away, but your Mr. Know-It-All hit a raw nerve. Or maybe I needed to give myself a pep talk . . . to remind myself of things I know in my bones but tend to forget when irritations get out of hand.

Anyhow, I'm sure we'll straighten out the mess somehow. We have to. It's just a matter of time.

All my love,
*Zippy*

## Haifa Bay

### November 3, 1948

Dearest Mother, Dad and Naomi,

Just heard the election returns. Truman did it again. How did that happen?

There is a real mail mix-up. I write, you write, and nobody has been getting anybody's letters. I just received a two-month-old airmail V-letter from you opened by an Arab censor. Someone read me the Arabic wording on the censor's stub: it says "Egypt." So that answers that. What probably happens is that mail destined for Israel sent via commercial airlines is detained for censorship, if not by the Egyptians then by the Israelis. Everybody is interested in finding out what the enemy knows.

Am enjoying Haifa's quiet, dignified atmosphere. Glad I changed. My new assignment is working out fine. Been given a room to myself and the boys on the base are helping fix it up. The electrician made me a lamp; the carpenter, a chest of drawers; the Sergeant Major had the place scrubbed up and the gardener sent flowers. Last night the Air Force band put on a jazz session and I danced my feet off.

The doctor I work with is originally from Czechoslovakia, an interesting person, young, very sound bedside approach, no *shvitz* (hot air) about him at all, with a sense of humor and a love of the unroutine — a kind of free spirit. Much to my liking. He lets me run the show. I've made a schedule of what should be done by whom which leaves us both enough time to go on routine visits to the various installations in Haifa under our supervision or scamper off to town.

Am at the airport . . . love to watch the big silver streamlined planes soar in and land and look at the bewildered, smiling or uncertain faces of the people alighting. Sometimes I find someone I know, sometimes I don't. Wish I could stow away on an outward-bound flight without all the to-do's of passports and visas; fly to I don't care where — U.S., Europe. Just for the hell and excitement of it. But, no such luck, my nearest, farthest and only flight will be to Tel Aviv or thereabouts. The noise is deafening — United Nations and Air France planes buzzing all over the place.

Stopped long enough to give bear hugs to a group of our boys just returned from pilot training school abroad. I knew them from Jerusalem. We drank a *"Lechaim"* on orange juice and wished ourselves and the world well.

It has been such an exhilarating day. So much happening. I dash from control room, to infirmary, to immigration office and on and on to coordinate, follow up, etc. Of course, this isn't La Guardia Airport, nor even Lydda, but it is one of the liveliest airfields in the Middle East right now. Only, in case the censor is looking over my shoulder, I won't mention its name.

Just arranged for this letter to go off on the next plane. Postage, incidentally, is now up to seventy mils — the equivalent of a cup of coffee in a swanky cafe or two cakes in a sidewalk kiosk or half a package of cigarettes.

Love,
*Zippy*

*Jaffa*

*November 9, 1948*

Dearest Mother, Dad and Naomi,

The world looks very bright tonight as I lie here in Rachie's bed in Jaffa, my hair in pin curls and my face smeared generously with Ponds cream. Haifa, the war, the world — out of mind, out of sight . . . for a day.

I was calmly attending to my usual routine when I heard an unfamiliar motor warming up on the field and dashed to the roof to see what was happening. Simultaneously, there was a hurry-up phone call. "Grab your toothbrush, get a pass and come over quickly with a big smile showing." The boys at flight control were looking after my interests.

I was ready in a jiffy. Pass in pocket, found a motorcycle hitch to the field and was ready for action. The smile, I found out, was to be used on two Air France pilots who are not supposed to take military personnel on flights. But, well, you know.

So, up I went — forty empty seats, the crew and me. It turned out to be not just a jaunt to Lydda airport — a twenty-minute flight — as I was led to believe, but a test-something flight that took an hour and cruised us over almost the entire country. Golly, it was terrific looking down at the rolling hills and dots of houses — a Monopoly board. The sea was a blue mirror with white mist floating over it, like whipped-cream peaks. Nine thousand feet into the sun, over the sands of the Negev and the stretches of brown crusty earth with occasional patches of green.

Of course, I was almost arrested at Lydda, but I had adequate papers and a perfect right to hitchhike by air — there's no law against it — even if it did set a new precedent about where, how and with whom. In the end, the police were even nice enough to get me a ride straight to Jaffa where I had to report.

Bumped into an old army buddy who tells me that the *Machal* office (the authority which deals with overseas volunteers) had a search party out to find me. Wanted to assign me to an English-language Army magazine or newspaper that is being organized. Glad I haven't been forgotten but somebody should have told them I've been posted to Haifa — and like it there.

Love,
*Zippy*

## Haifa Bay

### November 15, 1948

Dear Everbody,

The winter has set in suddenly and definitely. The first tropical rains. Then, without warning, the sun peeps out and beats down with a vengeance. Everything about this country is unpredictable.

We've opened the hospital; there is so much to do. This morning was one hectic but orderly confusion. Had to give the entire base vaccinations against small pox. You never saw so many great big heroes turn green at the sight of a white apron and some alcohol. Anyhow, all finished and accounted for. I even managed to get to the airport to finish the vaccinations there. Wish to heck the doctor would get back — he's really missed. One day on leave and everything happens just when he's not around.

Went to Haifa the other day to order some supplies. On the way back, happened to be passing the Bahai Persian Gardens on Mount Carmel. My driver, in the airport's jeep, wanted to show me the sights, so we stopped in for a quick tour and heard a lecture on Bahaism — a Chicago money man supports the cult. Spacious temples, hidden rooms and crevices. Have to remove your shoes and tread Persian carpets petaled with flowers and sprayed with spiced aromas. Very solemn stuff.

The Doc just came back from Tel Aviv with the wonderful news that we are getting a brand new ambulance. Probably American, with the huge Magen David Adom insignia and "B'nai B'rith Lodge number so-and-so" or "The Ladies Garment Workers' Union" painted on it in oversize letters. I think they would be very upset if they knew that the Army repaints its ambulances brown — so you no longer get socked in the eye by the donor's name. But, name or no name, they are much appreciated.

I can't get used to the fact that not everyone in uniform is marching to the same drum as I am. I was too starry-eyed to notice them — the shirkers and the war profiteers who are about as lit up with patriotism as a shattered neon sign.

Talking with people, and I do plenty of that, I can't help noticing the types we have been getting in the grab-bag collection of new immigrants that have come from all corners of the earth. So many types, you can become a student of human nature.

A guy comes in for a change of bandage or an aspirin and stays an hour telling you what he thinks about everything. Or else he doesn't and makes you feel that he wants to talk — so you drag it out of him. Some of these people are very hard to take, maybe because a lot of their humanity has been kicked out of them in every country they were booted in and out of. To survive, they learned all the tricks: some steal as naturally as they breathe.

Or take a girl, like one of my assistants, French by way of Poland, Germany and lots of persecution, who thinks that women have really only one function and nursing is something one does in the daytime while waiting to perform the real function after hours. To her, right and wrong are as interchangeable as hot and cold water when you mix them.

I am trying hard to accept the "humankind" I find here. I really don't like some of them but I pity them, have to tolerate them and try to understand them. It takes all kinds to make a nation.

Love,
*Zippy*

*Haifa Bay*

*November 20, 1948*

Dear All,

Been having some trouble with a tooth lately and haven't had a chance to take care of it. The other day, it became swollen and painful. I went to the Army dentist, waited my turn like a good soldier and then, after an hour, got fed up. So, in my best English — the only *protectzia* I can summon — I explained that I was the camp nurse on duty and would they please take me without further waiting.

If I had known what was inside, I wouldn't have insisted so hard. Three sorry looking characters were leaning over three sorrier looking characters, drilling away intently. I was steered to the nearest chair. I explain my problem. The dentist calls over his two associates . . . "American job," they concur. They prattle away in German for a few minutes and then my man comes at me with a chisel. As he nears the finish line, he calmly informs me that he can remove the crown and, perhaps, deal with the inflammation but he doubts if he can put it back on again . . . also, the Army doesn't do extensive dental work unless the damage was directly related to a war injury. At which point, I reached hurriedly for my jacket and smiled my way backwards out of the room.

Inquired at the *Machal* office and was given the address of a good dentist. When I got there, I found myself in a room filled with glass eyes staring me in the face. Thought I was in the wrong place. It turns out that this was the doctor's day for fitting soldiers for artificial eyes.

"My hobby," he told me.

Three days a week he's a dentist, two days a week a general practitioner at the Army hospital, one day a week a surgeon and, in between, he has a private practice which he says covers anything from a broken heart, broken tooth, athlete's foot to extracting shell fragments.

I only found out after I left his office that he actually does all those things and is considered an expert in each. He also knows how to deal with patients. The waiting room was filled with guys, each with one eye covered. I felt sort of out of place with both my eyes where they ought to be. The boys were all feeling sorry for someone who had just left the room who had lost both hands as well as an eye.

As I was trying to sneak out of the room unseen — I figured a tooth didn't need this doctor's attention as long as he was involved in more important things — the doc spied me and called me into his hobby room. For a while, I watched his deft fingers molding eyes and then I sort of blurted out that I had thought he was a dentist. He was in a very good mood, left his plastic to cool and steered me toward the ominous drill chair. Took a quick, efficient look, yanked off the crown, smeared the inside with medication and cement and stuffed it back in place.

"Come back in about two days," says he, "for treatment, and to keep me company, whenever you like."

I haven't seen his bill yet but whatever it will be, it'll be well worth it three times over. What a charming guy and really knows his job. Too bad he isn't with our clinic.

On the way out, the boys in the waiting room joked a bit. They wanted to know which of my eyes was plastic.

"Take it out and put it on the table. We've got a bet on."

I almost wished I had one to remove, so as not to disappoint them.

*Zippy*

## Haifa Bay

*November 29, 1948*

Dearest Mother, Dad and Naomi,

From the roof of the hospital, I watched this morning's parade, a parade of soldiers of the Jewish State. Not partisans or underground fighters. Soldiers, standing erect and proud, in rain puddles six inches deep, wearing shabby outfits — winter uniforms still haven't reached us — listening to lofty words of accomplishment and tribute.

I, too, listened but my thoughts wandered — drifted back to last November 29th, 1947, Jerusalem, the courtyard of the Sochnut building, the spontaneous joy that filled the streets when the United Nations resolution calling for a Jewish State was approved.

And now we march, we form ranks, we listen to speeches, we salute officers: Natan, as they taught him in the Russian army; Lev, as he learned in the RAF; Aryeh, as they do in the Polish army; Uzi (the Sabra), reluctantly; Moshe, in Turkish style. All of them, saluting the Jewish Officer in Command, representing *Tzva Haganah LeYisrael* (Israel Defense Forces). The same people who were partisans last year are soldiers today, and civilian citizens of the State of Israel tomorrow. I wondered whether "tomorrow" would be another year or an eternity?

The command rang out, *"Chofshi"* (dismissed). The ranks broke to the count of three and everyone dashed to the canteen where they mimicked each other marching, saluting and even drinking tea. Nobody mentioned the words we had heard, nobody referred to the historic importance of the day or the momentous events that had transpired, transforming us into a State with an Army. Nobody marveled at the wonder of it all. Were these miracles already being taken for granted?

For me, this pathetic parade was a fulfillment, a consummation. I kept thinking that it had been mustered from all the lands of the world, had taken not one year but *two thousand years* to materialize. Next year, the parade will probably be more impressive. We'll have smart uniforms, everyone will salute in the same way, stand in straight lines and know all the marching commands. We will have learned so much and, possibly, forgotten so much.

The talk in the canteen was about leave time, the latest movie, tonight's party, who has an extra blanket or what's the biggest gripe of the day. I looked at the faces of those around me and thought of the patriots who had fought the American Revolution. Faced with a Fourth of July celebration 1948–style, would they have the same sober thoughts I was having?

Like everything else here, it has happened very fast, too fast — the twenty-ninth of November is just a red-letter day on the calendar. A fighting people hasn't time to be sentimental.

But I couldn't help thinking of Moshe, Oded, Zvi, Amnon, Yaakov, Aryeh, Matty, Nachum and a hundred others in Jerusalem, who a year ago danced and sang through the night with me, but didn't live long enough; they fell before the dream came true. The lump in my throat was too big in my mouth.

Was it only a year ago? No, it was worlds ago, each a separate world: the University, the Haganah, Deir Yassin, the Burma Road, Sheikh Jarrah, Katamon, Talpiot, Tel Aviv, Haifa — worlds of people, places and events.

I can't believe this year. So much has happened, but the most important thing by far is the birth of the State. I've been part of it and it will forever be part of me. I guess that means I am telling you I intend to see this war through and then remain on, whatever happens. This is now my HOME.

Love,
*Zippy*

Some months later, with the war at a formal truce, I was assigned to *Ma'arachot*, the Army Publications Department, to collect material for a book on Mickey Marcus, the American West Point colonel who had served in Israel's War of Independence and been killed in a mishap. My job was to interview anyone who had had contact with him while their impressions were still fresh: from his lady driver to the man who had recruited him and up the ranks to the Prime Minister himself, David Ben-Gurion.

Toward the end of 1949, I returned to the States intending to wind up my affairs before settling in Israel permanently, but found myself caught up in a new framework — the Israel Foreign Office. Asked to serve as executive secretary to Arthur Lourie, the consul general in New York, I worked at the consulate for about a year.

At the first Israeli reception in honor of the first Israeli foreign minister, Moshe Sharett (attending the United Nations General Assembly), my duty as hostess was to greet the guests and SMILE. That was the day I met my husband-to-be, Israel's assistant military attaché who — as the family story goes — took the smile seriously. Our wedding at the Israeli Embassy in Washington, D.C. was the first "diplomatic" event of its kind. The Best Man was Colonel Chaim Herzog, then military attaché, now President of the State of Israel.

We returned to Israel in 1952 and settled in Zahalah, where our two sons were born and raised. In the early sixties, the family moved to Savyon which was being built by my husband, a civil engineer, for a major development company.

Along with the rest of Israel, I have lived through the difficult, fascinating, formative years of the state, as well as the wars that beset it: the Sinai Campaign (1956), when, frustrated, I stayed home tending the babies while my husband was mobilized; the Six-Day War (1967), when my sons were old enough to dig trenches and distribute milk, mail and messages; the Yom Kippur War (1973), when our younger son was a cadet in the Air Force pilot training course and the elder in a commando unit on the Southern Front; and, during the war in Lebanon (1982), when even my not-so-young lieutenant colonel husband was called up. Enough of wars.

Throughout the years, I have worked professionally as a free-lance editor, translator and publications production consultant. I was the first editor of the national Bulletin of the Association of Americans and Canadians in Israel.

* * *

When I wrote the letters reproduced in this book I didn't expect to be rereading them forty years later. In my wildest reveries, as I was growing up in New York, I never imagined that I would see the Zionist dream of a Jewish State materialize in my own lifetime or that I would personally take part in making it come true. Nor could I have anticipated the wondrous achievements of the state, nor the changes — some of them troubling — that have marked its development.

I cannot really be objective after all these years of living at boiling point in a melting pot, with the tensions, frustrations and irritations of everyday life and the constant turmoil of wars and their aftermath. For me, they are part of life here, part of the challenge.

People today, especially young people, sometimes forget that only a few short decades ago *there was no Jewish State*, no Israel. It didn't exist. They take it for granted. But for those of us who were privileged to take part in its birth, Israel will always have a special aura. It was a turning point not only in the history of our people, but in our personal lives as well.

What I discovered in my first year here is still true. I belong here. This is my home. I am still a starry-eyed optimist who believes that whatever we do here as individuals is meaningful. We count just by *being here*, helping to bring closer the dream of a better Israel. My commitment to this country is still a source of personal satisfaction. Then, as now, I know why I am here.